GOOD CHRISTIAN MEN

HENRY MARTIN P. DAVIDSON

D1576289

Essay Index Reprint Series

BOOKS FOR LIBRARIES PRESS
FREEPORT, NEW YORK

INTERNATIONAL STANDARD BOOK NUMBER:
0-8369-2390-1

LIBRARY OF CONGRESS CATALOG CARD NUMBER:
70-142616

PRINTED IN THE UNITED STATES OF AMERICA

To the Memory of

G. M. B.

S. S. D.

T. K. N.

"Good Christian Men"

who

"by their example and encouragement

have helped us on

our way."

PREFACE

"The secret of the influence of any society never lies so much in its rules or constitution as in the personality of its founder. The rules and the constitution are at best only an attempt to organize and perpetuate the secret of a man's or of men's grasp of spiritual things, be they political or religious."

H. B. Washburn, *Men of Conviction*, pp. 87–88.

THIS BOOK sets out to tell, as simply as possible, the life story of several conspicuous Christians, and to estimate their influence and importance, both in their own time and through the years that follow. Of necessity it will also be concerned with the conditions that produced these men, as well as with the cultural and civilizing influence of Christianity. The biographical method has been chosen chiefly because, as Dean Washburn suggests, the best way to understand and put a value on any institution or movement is to see what quality of men it has produced. If it can be shown that some men have been set on fire by Jesus Christ and have made some difference in their world, it will have been enough. For what is Christianity but such personal loyalty to Him, and such personal witness in the world of men?

In quotations from the Bible the various English translations have been drawn upon, but they have been adapted, and, in the New Testament passages, translations have been made from the original Greek. The author takes all blame for errors in fact and in opinion, but at the same time he acknowledges with gratitude the assistance of the many friends and critics, who have persuaded him to go on with this book, and have pointed out some of the shortcomings as it progressed, especially the Reverend F. F. Bartrop, the Reverend H. D. Gasson, and the Reverend C. T. Webb, former colleagues at St. Paul's School, Concord, N. H.; Miss Marjorie True Gregg who reads with a careful eye, Doctor Erdman Harris of Lawrenceville School, Mrs. Belle B. Richardson, late of St. Paul's School, Miss Cornelia V. B. Kimball of Concord, and Mr. Robert E. Bacon of St. George's School for assistance in reading the proof and preparing the Index. The author also remembers with gratitude those former pupils, too numerous to mention, on whom the material was first tried out, and who contributed more than they knew in suggestion and criticism. They had some of the qualities of "Good Christian Men."

H. Martin P. Davidson.

St. George's School,
Newport, Rhode Island,
October, 1940.

CONTENTS

GOOD CHRISTIAN MEN

Chapter 1

GOOD CHRISTIAN MEN

"The goodly fellowship of the Prophets"

BACK OF ALL good Christian men stand a long story and a great tradition. Though it may sound contradictory, Christianity began long before Christ was born in Bethlehem. Christianity began in the mind and purposes of God. "God so loved the world" that, before He sent His Son, He began to plan and work to win the love of men, and draw them into fellowship with Himself. The story of how this was done is found in what is called the Old Testament, and proves a stumbling-block to many people. Old Testament characters seem crude and often immoral, their religion primitive and mercenary, their attitude toward other peoples narrow and nationalistic. Much may be said for this judgment, but Christians cannot be content with it. For Christ said of the Old Testament "I came not to destroy but to fulfill." Moreover He quoted two texts drawn from that source as the summary of His teachings, "Thou shalt love the Lord thy God with all thy heart and with all thy soul and with all thy mind" and "Thou shalt love thy neighbor as thyself," and He added "On these two commandments hang all the Law and the Prophets." The Jewish Scripture or, as we say, the Old Testament is still called by the Jews "The Law, the Prophets, and the

1

Writings." Christ, using the common shortened form of
the title, was saying that in the Old Testament are to be
found the deepest purposes of God, and that out of the
Old Testament could be drawn principles sufficient for
the highest life of men. He was saying further that these
writings, and the Jewish religion contained in them,
formed the foundation of the Christian faith and character.

It is a mistake, however, to think of Jewish Scripture,
or of Christian for that matter, as we think of the Koran of
Mohammed. That sacred book was produced by one man
within a few years, and is all of one piece. Mohammed,
influenced by the debased Jewish and Christian writings
that he knew as well as by the primitive Arabian religion
which he had practiced, composed the Koran after his
mind was made up; and he said in final form what he
wanted to say. It is not so with the Old Testament. For
several hundred years, five hundred at least, it was being written, while the oral traditions go back of that,
and are derived from other than strictly Jewish sources.
In the text itself in its completed form various strata can
be traced. To take one example, there are two distinct
accounts of Creation in the early chapters of Genesis,
both of them influenced by the Babylonian and kindred
accounts. The earlier one (beginning in the middle of
the fourth verse of chapter two), gives a picture of God
acting much as a man, "walking in the garden in the cool
of the day," even experimenting in finding a proper
mate for the man He has made. In the later narrative
(chapter one and the beginning of chapter two), God is
majestic, all-knowing, all-powerful, Creator of heaven and
earth. In the early books of the Old Testament scholars
find as many as four such strata, each one with its own

peculiarities of style and outlook, as well as its own moral standards and theology. The Old Testament is a composite collection of religious literature, held together solely by the conviction that God has been at work among the people and in the institutions described. It is not surprising therefore that the religious beliefs and practices and the moral standards do not move on one level.

Neither time nor the varying literary and religious traditions, however, were the chief factors in the formation of the Old Testament. That place belongs to the prophets, beginning with Amos in the eighth century before Christ. The word prophet literally means one who speaks forth on behalf of some one else; the Jews used it in the sense of one who speaks for God, any idea of foretelling the future was entirely secondary, if it was present at all. Moses and Joshua and their early leaders were called the former prophets, and Amos and his successors were therefore known as the latter prophets. The first of the latter prophets lived and worked before the historical narratives were put into their present form, in fact they were often responsible for the particular form and emphasis of the narratives. More important than that, the prophets were responsible for the strong moral insistence in the Hebrew religion as well as for the conviction that the God of Israel was the God of all men and that Israel's mission was to tell others about Him. Yet the prophets were not simply discovering these truths in a kind of religious laboratory by the unaided strength of their minds or intellects. They were thinking God's thoughts after Him, or as Amos put it, "The Lord God hath spoken, who can but tell it forth to others?" (Amos 3:8.)

The Jews accepted this development of ideas, and

tried to live by it, but they found difficulty in the idea of the mission to the rest of the world. They took pride in being the Chosen People, the People they always called themselves, and they seemed to forget that they were chosen for a purpose, chosen to carry out a task. In a sense both history and geography were against them. They had always to struggle against odds to maintain their national and religious life, and little wonder if the struggle absorbed them. That struggle was part of their training and discipline, however, as the prophet whom we call the Second Isaiah tried to show them in his poems about the "Suffering Servant of the Lord." Writing from exile in Babylonia around the year 550 B.C., he held that the purposes of God for men could only be realized if the people He had chosen were willing to pay the price—that is to face opposition and possible defeat, and to accept the consequent suffering. In the beginning God had made man a free agent, free to accept or reject His demands, and man had chosen to reject them. The people of Israel had done so again and again, the nations of men had done the same; but God was not to be balked. The exile in Babylon, the destruction of Jerusalem and the Temple, the despair and hardships, were not only punishment for disloyalty, they were also God's means of bringing the people to see their true place among the nations. Out of the suffering was to emerge a new sense of purpose:

"Behold my servant, whom I uphold; my chosen in whom my soul delighteth: I have put my spirit upon him; he shall bring forth judgment to the nations. . . . He shall not fail nor be discouraged till he have set judgment in the earth. . . . I, the Lord, have called thee in righteousness, and will hold thine hand and will keep thee and give thee for a covenant of the people, for a light of the Gentiles; to open the blind eyes, to bring out the prisoners from the dungeon, and them that sit in darkness out of the prison house. . . . It is too light a thing that thou shouldest be my servant, to raise up the tribes of Jacob and to restore the redeemed of Israel; I will also give thee for a light to the Gentiles that my salvation may be unto the ends of the earth!" (Isaiah 42:1, 4, 6, 7; 49:6).

"He was despised and rejected of men; a man of sorrows and acquainted with grief; and as one from whom men hide their face he was despised, and we esteemed him not. Surely he hath borne our griefs and carried our sorrows . . . it pleased the Lord to bruise him . . . by his knowledge shall my righteous servant make many righteous." (Isaiah 53:3, 4, 10a, 11b.)

The task was too hard. It demanded more than the nation would give. Israel forgot that God could and would bring victory out of defeat, though that experience was written large on the pages of her history, and she chose to ignore His will for her. She resented the discipline and the suffering, and rejected the mission. Some one else must be found therefore who would accept them since God's will for men must be accomplished. "God so loved the world that He gave His only begotten Son" (John 3:16) is the Christian Gospel, the *good news* about God. The discipline and the mission of the people of Israel were accepted by Christ as God's way of winning men to Himself. The Suffering Servant was fulfilled in Jesus. And since "the servant is not greater than his Lord" this discipline and this mission are also the credentials of all good Christian men. This is the tradition in which Christ's followers must stand.

Chapter 2

PAUL OF TARSUS

"New occasions teach new duties"

A PRISONER OF IMPERIAL ROME was being cross-examined. On the judgment seat sat the governor, and beside him a native ruler, king-by-courtesy of a near-by region. Rome's power and authority were further represented by soldiers of her legions and the governor's legal advisers. At the bar stood a short man, with a squint in his eye perhaps, obviously a Jew. Ordinarily Rome would not have gone to so much trouble for a prisoner snatched from a mob's fury. But this man, it seemed, was not merely a Jew, he was also a citizen of the Empire. As such he had refused to be tried in Jerusalem, where the religious authorities of his own people wanted to prefer a religious charge against him. He maintained that he had committed no offense against his nation or his God, and he claimed the rights of any Roman citizen, a review of his case before Cæsar's tribunal in Rome itself. The governor was embarrassed at having no definite charge to send along with the prisoner. Happily for him at this point, there came to pay his respects a petty local ruler, a king in name, Herod Agrippa descended from the great Herod; and to him the

6

governor turned for help. He would know intimately about Jewish affairs, and maybe would find ground for a political charge.

Rarely however had a cross-examination so completely been in the hands of the man being examined. From the moment he was given leave to speak, his was the voice of authority. His words and the strength of his conviction carried all who heard before him. Once the governor interrupted, saying the prisoner talked as if he were mad. And the king-by-courtesy in sarcasm remarked that the prisoner would soon persuade himself of that farthest of all possibilities, that he had converted the king. None of this dampened his zeal. He had been born a Jew, he said, and had been strictly brought up as a Pharisee, zealous for the law of Moses, and foremost in opposing the followers of that prophet of Nazareth called Jesus. In this he had felt himself to be doing the right thing. But one day, "as he came to Damascus," he saw clearly that what he had been fighting as falsehood was in reality the truth. In Eastern fashion he spoke of a light from heaven at midday and a voice from the cloud. Yet even in that law court it was clear what he meant. Now he was foremost among those who tried to win others to this *way*. He was convinced that he was born for this purpose, and as Christ's "ambassador in bonds" he must speak, whatever befell him. Neither the governor nor his guest could find in this a charge to send to Cæsar. Nor could they see much of lasting importance in it. Yet before long wherever their prisoner had already told his story, even in Rome itself, whither they must send him, men and women held to the same faith and followed the same way of life in the face of torture and violent death. No one was so much responsible for this result as Paul of Tarsus, their prisoner. More than any one else he made it possible for Christianity to become the religion of Europeans.

Christianity began, and the fact is sometimes forgotten, in an Asiatic province of the Roman Empire, among a people despised generally by Europeans. It was a Jewish cult. Jesus of Nazareth, its founder, had been a Jew, and its earliest adherents were Jews. The Jewish authorities, to be sure, had secured the death of Jesus, chiefly because his teaching seemed to them to be destructive of the religion of their fathers. Nevertheless, neither Jewish opponents nor Jewish followers supposed that the teaching would appeal to non-Jews. In the first chapters of the Acts of the Apostles, the only account we have of the early days of Christianity, the intensely Jewish character of the first Christians is clearly brought out. The very first thing the Disciples did, after the Ascension of Jesus, was to elect one to take the place of Judas among the Twelve. They were expecting an immediate return of Jesus as the Jewish Messiah, God's Anointed One, *Christos* in Greek; and the Apostles were to be heads of the twelve tribes of the new Israel. Jesus, the Messiah, had come to fulfill the ancient promises made by God to Israel, and no one could partake of that fulfillment who did not belong to the house of Israel either by birth or by adoption. Christians were still loyal to the law of Moses, they still went to the Temple for prayers and the sacrifices, and thought of themselves as strict Jews (Acts 5:42); they simply added to this their belief that Messiah had come and would soon come again.

Once Peter opened the way for Gentiles, that is, non-

Jews, to enter the fellowship without entering the commonwealth of Israel. But the door was not allowed to stay open. Cornelius, a Roman officer, who had been deeply influenced by the Jewish faith and may have considered becoming a Proselyte, a Jew by adoption, asked Peter why he could not be baptized. The answer was obvious, that he must first become a Jew, but it was not given because Peter felt that God had warned him in a vision not to refuse Cornelius' request. So Peter baptized him, but he had to assure the Christian community in Jerusalem that he did not consider this baptism of one who was not a Jew as a precedent (Acts 10 and 11:1–18). It was a special case.

Another point of view soon makes itself felt, however, among the disciples of Jesus. Some Hellenists or Grecian Jews, either by birth or adoption, who had lived among the Gentiles had come back to Jerusalem and joined the fellowship of Jesus the Messiah. Friction soon arose over the distribution of food to the poor among the Christian group. The Hellenists said that they were being discriminated against. To prevent a recurrence of this charge seven men were chosen, all of whom had Greek names though only one is called a Proselyte, who are usually spoken of as the Seven Deacons (Acts 6:1–6). The leader was Stephen, and he drew the fire of the Jewish authorities who accused him of saying that "Jesus of Nazareth will destroy this place [*i.e.* the Temple], and change the customs of Moses" (Acts 6:14). The charge was not sustained, but he was stoned to death, thus becoming the first martyr, and his friends and followers among the Hellenist group were forced to flee, though the Apostles were not molested.

Some of these Hellenists, coming to Antioch in Syria, admitted Greeks into the fellowship without requiring that they become Jews (Acts 11:20). When news of this departure in practice reached the Apostles in Jerusalem a man was sent out to investigate, perhaps to put a stop to the proceedings. His name was Barnabas. He was impressed rather than upset by what he found in Antioch. "When he came and saw the grace of God he was glad and encouraged them all" (Acts 11:23). Immediately he "went to Tarsus to look for Saul, and when he found him he brought him to Antioch where they stayed for a year with the church" (Acts 11:26). Apparently both Barnabas and Saul felt that there was nothing disturbing in what was happening in Antioch, and their feeling was confirmed after they had toured certain Greek cities of Asia Minor. They had spoken first in each of these cities to Jews, had been howled down or driven from the synagogues because they said that Jesus had come to save all men, not Jews only; then they had turned to Gentiles, who gladly accepted their teaching. Christian groups, made up largely of these Gentiles, were to be found in all these cities (Acts 13:42–43, 48–50). Barnabas and Saul, or Paul as we shall henceforth call him, therefore saw no reason for demanding that their converts first become Jews. To become a Jew by adoption one must promise to keep certain regulations which seemed to Gentiles to have little to do with religion, such as the refusal to eat pork or other "unclean" meat. Moreover a man had to undergo circumcision, a rite which aroused opposition among Greeks and Romans, and henceforth as a member of a despised race, he was cut off from his former social connections. Few Gentiles were willing to meet these demands, and they soon appeared to Paul and Barnabas to be irrelevant.

The question was not settled so easily however. When Paul and Barnabas returned to Antioch, where the disciples were already being called "Christians" (Acts 11:26), they found the Gentile converts there genuinely upset because some had come to them from Jerusalem, saying that unless they were circumcised as the Jewish law demanded they could not be members of the Christian fellowship. Paul and Barnabas, fresh from their experience of Greeks accepting Christ gladly, would not admit this contention. Accordingly they went to Jerusalem to settle the question and, though they met opposition at first, after relating their experiences the final decision was in their favor (Acts 14:27–15:20). A letter containing this decision was written to the Gentile Christians: "The apostles and presbyters in the fellowship to the brothers who are Gentiles in Antioch and Syria and Cilicia: Greetings: As we have learned that some of our number, unauthorized by us, have upset you by their teaching and unsettled your souls, we have unanimously agreed to select some of our number and send them to you with our dearly beloved Paul and Barnabas, who have risked their lives for the sake of our Lord Jesus Christ. Therefore we send Judas and Silas to you with this message, which they will also give to you by word of mouth. The Holy Spirit guiding us, we have decided not to put upon you any burden apart from this essential requirement: keep yourselves from food that has been offered to idols, from the tasting of blood, from the meat of animals which have been strangled, and from immorality" (Acts 15:23–29).

There may have been some who did not understand the full implications of this decision, but by corporate action the Christians in Jerusalem had given sanction to Paul to carry on as he had begun. Jesus had said, "Go ye into ALL the world," "make disciples of ALL nations," and it was Paul who, though he had neither seen nor heard his Master on earth, caught the full significance of these words. It was Paul who saw summed up in Christ the real mission of Israel, which Israel had rejected as it had Christ. The people had been chosen for a task, "to be a light to lighten the Gentiles," but they had chosen to keep the treasure for themselves instead. That was what Paul saw with such force on the Damascus road, and with it the necessity for every Christian to do what Israel had refused to do.

We know very little about Paul's early years. In a letter written much later to a group of Greek Christians in the town of Philippi he wrote: "I belonged to the people of Israel, to the tribe of Benjamin. I was a Jew, the son of Jewish parents. In regard to the Law [of Moses] I was a Pharisee" (Philippians 3:5). References in his speeches as recorded in the later chapters of Acts add little to this. He was born in Tarsus, chief city of the Roman Province of Cilicia in Asia Minor, and educated in Jerusalem, probably to become a rabbi. He spoke both Greek and Hebrew, the latter meaning the Aramaic dialect of Hebrew in common use among Palestinian Jews of the day, though he must also have known the classical Hebrew of the Sacred Scriptures. He boasted that he was a Roman citizen by birth, which meant that his father had acquired citizenship. Like every Jew he could practice a trade, his being tent-making.

He boasted later on that only once had he accepted the charity of others and not earned his own living (Philippians 4:15–16, I Thessalonians 2:9). His Jewish name, Saul, came from his family connection with the tribe of Benjamin, whence the first king of his nation had also sprung. Paul, his Roman name, probably came from the Roman official through whom his father had acquired citizenship. A Jew who was a Roman citizen would customarily take a Roman name for legal and business use. In the letter to the Philippians mentioned above it is possible to find the suggestion that he had not always been dependent on his own labors, and had either renounced his wealth or been cut off by his family when he became a Christian. "I know how to live with little, I know how to live with much. I have been let into the secret of all kinds and conditions of life, to enjoy plenty and to suffer hunger, to live in prosperity and in want" (Philippians 4:12). We know from the Acts that he was present and approved of the stoning of Stephen: "The witnesses [of Stephen's death] laid their clothes at the feet of a young man named Saul" (Acts 7:58). In the letter to the Galatian Christians, he recalled his early hostility to Christians. "You know of my past life in Judaism, how furiously I persecuted the Church of God and made havoc in it, and how I outdid many of my own age among my fellows in my zeal for the religious traditions of my fathers" (Galatians 1:13–14).

Is there anything in these few facts to explain his later career? Tarsus was "no mean city" as he said, being an important commercial center with a fine harbor, and having a University excelling in some respects even Athens and Alexandria. Paul had absorbed naturally some of the at-

mosphere of this Greek speaking city, just as he had learned
the language by daily use, but it is unlikely that as a
pious Jew he attended the heathen schools. He would have
known Greeks personally and individually, some of them
perhaps as friends and companions, an experience one born
and brought up in Jerusalem could not have had. His
figures of speech were essentially those of a city man; he
thought and spoke in terms of the market place and the
price of a slave, of soldiers' armor and warfare, of the
games in the Greek stadium. But these things are only
part of the story. Paul would have called them incidental.
The important thing to his mind was "when God chose
to reveal his Son to me" (Galatians 1:15–16).

The account of how he became a Christian occurs three
times in the Acts, once as a narrative and twice in his
speeches (Acts 9:1–21, 22:5–22, 26:2–18). Paul was on his
way to Damascus to bring charges against Christians there.
Suddenly he discovered that his zeal was being spent in
the wrong direction, that to find the true way of life he
must follow, not persecute, Christ. This discovery was a
spiritual turning point for him which could not be put into
human language, because such experiences never can be
adequately expressed. The events could hardly have been
as sudden as the story suggests, as Paul recognized when
he wrote to the Galatians that God "set me apart from
my birth." All his life had prepared him for and had led
up to this event. Doubts had already begun to form in his
mind; his part in persecution already touched his conscience. He started to Damascus to quiet his doubts and
fears in a life of action, only to find them growing more
powerful as he rode. Finally in a very spasm of groping

he found the light, found rather that the light had pursued him all the while. Thenceforward he was willing, even anxious to proclaim the change in himself in Damascus or elsewhere. But, as he was careful to say in the letter to the Galatians, he did not go to Jerusalem until three years later, and then only for two weeks' private consultation with Peter and James, "the brother of the Lord," who was looked on as leader of the group there. From the start he was sure that his peculiar mission was to preach Christ to the Gentiles. Perhaps Barnabas knew of this conviction when he sought Paul's aid in Antioch.

The best summary of Paul's life as a Christian is to be found in his own words, "I have been often in danger of death; five times I was given the forty lashes (less one) by the Jews, three times I have been beaten by the Romans, once stoned, three times shipwrecked, adrift at sea for a day and a night; in my constant travelling I have been in danger of rivers and of robbers, in danger from Jew and Gentile, in danger in towns and in the desert, on the sea and among false brothers . . . in labors and in hardships, through many a sleepless night, in hunger and in thirst, without food often, cold and lacking clothing" (II Corinthians 11:24–27). Or as he wrote near the end of his life, "I have fought the good fight, I have finished the course, I have kept the faith" (II Timothy 4:7). It is a story of hardships suffered gladly "for Christ's sake." It is more than that, it is his song of triumph.

Some one has said that wherever Paul came there was either a riot or a revival. The riots can be read of in many places in the Acts. Jews in Thessalonica stirred up trouble and actually mobbed the house in which Paul stayed, drag-

ging out the owner and accusing him of treason to Rome
(Acts 17:1–13). In Corinth, where Paul stayed for eighteen months working at his trade, the Jewish opposition
took the form of accusing him before the Roman official.
But the pro-consul, Gallio, refused, as Rome usually did,
to take any side in a religious quarrel (Acts 18:1–17). At
Ephesus Paul came into conflict with the silversmiths, who
shrewdly based their opposition on religious grounds
though the grievance was economic. They said he was destroying the worship of Artemis (Diana), meaning that
he was ruining their trade in making and selling little
images of the goddess. The uproar was so great that Paul
was persuaded to remain indoors, and later to leave the
city secretly (Acts 19:23–20:1). In each of these places, as
in others, Paul left behind him a group of Christians, and
he kept in touch with each group by letters, called in the
New Testament the Epistles of St. Paul.

All this time Paul had watched the growing hostility
to him among his own people, the Jews, not only those
opposed to Christianity, but even many Jewish Christians.
They felt that he was playing false to their common background. He therefore decided to return to Jerusalem and
to show his personal loyalty to the religion of his upbringing by performing a Jewish purification vow in the Temple. This vow took seven days to perform. All went well
until on the last day he was attacked by a group of non-
Christian Jews from Ephesus. The tumult in the Temple
Court rose so shrill that the ever watchful Roman garrison
rushed to the scene. They rescued Paul, who astonished
the commander by asking in Greek if he might address
the mob. He was allowed to speak, which he did in the

ordinary Hebrew dialect, but he was howled down when he said that he was commissioned to take the message of Jesus to Gentiles. The Roman officer, puzzled by the proceedings, was about to examine him under the lash when Paul asserted his rights as a Roman citizen, an assertion which the officer at first was inclined to doubt. The Jews in the Council gave no clear statement of the disturbance; they merely fell to quarrelling among themselves. A plot to assassinate Paul was discovered by Paul's nephew (Acts 23:16), who is mentioned this one time only, and the prisoner was taken to the Roman governor's headquarters at Cæsarea on the coast. In the governor's court no charges save religious ones were brought, and Paul was held for safety and in hopes of a bribe (Acts 24:25–26) until a new governor came two years later.

It was the new governor who arranged the cross-examination of the prisoner with which this chapter opened. The governor, in order to win favor with the Jews, had proposed sending Paul to Jerusalem for trial. Paul knew that he could hardly expect to escape death there even if he was acquitted of the particular offense. Therefore as a Roman citizen he appealed to Cæsar. This meant he must be sent to Rome, a journey he had long desired to make (*cf.* Romans 1:11–13), only now the government itself must see that he arrived. The voyage was a stormy one and full of adventure (Acts 27 and 28). Finally the company reached Italy and Paul was met outside Rome by a group of Christians from the city where they seem already to have been fairly numerous. He was allowed to live in his own house, with a soldier to guard him, and to teach freely and without interruption. The book of Acts breaks off abruptly at this point, whether because the ending was lost or never written we do not know. An early tradition says that he was later released, and preached Christ to the "furthest confines of the West," and that finally he fell a victim to the persecution of Nero in the year 64 A.D.

Of the letters Paul wrote to groups of Christians in the cities he had visited, or to individual converts, thirteen have a place in our New Testament. It should be noted that in each case he wrote to meet a given situation without the faintest idea that the letters would be kept and read as Scripture. The very thought would have doubtless seemed sacrilege. Scripture to him meant the sacred writings of Israel, and he would not presume to write something to take place with them. Moreover it is hard to imagine him rounding off the phrases of his colloquial and not too polished Greek. He appears to have dictated to a scribe and then to have added the parting words in his own hand (*cf.* Galatians 6:11 or I Corinthians 16:21). The Christian community however very early came to treasure these letters and to feel that though addressed to one group at a given time they were applicable at any time. Unpolished though they may be, they reveal the inspiration of a poet and a thinker. The letter to the Galatians, for example, written in violent protest against forcing Gentile Christians to become Jews, literally burns with hot indignation, and has been called "the charter of Christian liberty." Such phrases as "there is neither Jew nor Greek, there is neither slave nor free . . . ye are all one in Christ," and "the fruit of the Spirit is love, joy, peace . . . against such there is no law," lift it above all place or time, though they were offhand utterances directed to simple people.

The key to Paul's greatness for Christian history lies in fact in the words to the Galatians, "There is neither Jew nor Greek . . . ye are all one in Christ." For Paul it was sufficient that a man be merely a man for him to be a Christian. The church in Jerusalem was inclined to think that a man must be a Jew first. In Paul's mind Christianity was the universal religion, the faith for all men of whatever race or station, and hence democratic and supernational. And as it was supernational so also was it supernatural. "Now you are the Body of Christ, and every one members of it" (I Corinthians 12:27). Paul felt that Christians must be in fact "members of Christ," bound to Him as parts of the body are to the whole. Isolated Christians and factions among Christians were contradictions in terms. The situation that called forth our First Epistle to the Corinthians is one of factions inside the local group, and Paul deals with it with irony bordering on sarcasm in his parable of the eye and the head that tried to secede from the hands and the feet (I Corinthians 12:21). The word "church" has been little used in this story, but it was never absent from the mind and speech of Paul, to whom it meant the new Israel transcending racial and national bounds, the true people of God aware of their mission to mankind, and of their essential membership with each other. The places Paul visited are those that one would find marked on any map of the Roman Empire, however small the scale, because they are the important places. He had an instinct for the strategic centers; there he must carry his message that Christ was for all men, and all men were meant for Christ. He was not content with the theory, he put it to work, and in so doing changed the religious history of Europe. Paul made it possible for Christianity to become a European religion and he stands among the founders of Western civilization.

Chapter 3

"IN THE FULNESS OF TIME
GOD SENT HIS SON"

THE WORDS which St. Paul used, in his letter to the Galatians (4:4) to express the readiness of Israel for Christ may also be used to describe the rest of the world. For though it seemed to be in religious confusion, in reality the world was waiting for Him. Men already had some idea of the things Christianity would teach in greater fulness. Men already craved the things Christianity could bring. "When men were prepared and in readiness God sent His Son."

The gods of Olympus, perhaps because they belonged to Olympus and not to the world, had nothing to say to the world's needs. At any rate educated Greeks and Romans no longer took them seriously, they regarded them merely as a personification of the forces of nature. Plato had seen them as magnified men and women, with lower standards of morals often than men themselves. Plato had seen further that behind all the gods of the Greek Pantheon there must be one Power or Force, which he called "Mind," and he thus opened the way for belief in one God. When, in the century before Christ, the Emperor Augustus revived the old religion of Greece the revival became no more than a patriotic gesture that ended in the deification of the Emperor himself. The common people held on to the worship of the old gods, primarily because of the festivals and holidays they provided. Our word "pagan," used to describe worshippers of the old gods, is probably derived from *paganus*, meaning a peasant, a countryman, and suggests that such worship lasted longest in the backwoods. The most serious failure on the part of the old religion of Greece was, as Plato saw, the separation of morals and religion. The high standards of early Rome lost their hold on men, and there was nothing in the worship of the gods of Olympus that demanded even a rudimentary morality. What a man did when once his sacrifice in the shrines was accomplished was no concern of the gods. The word profane means literally outside the shrine or temple, and has now the meaning of unreligious; it ought to mean also having no concern for morality.

The wars of conquest had opened up the West to Oriental influences, and among the strongest of these influences were the so-called Mystery Religions. The name "Mystery" came from the password or mystery that was revealed in secret rites of initiation, and was necessary to enter the life after death. This hope of immortality, which the Mysteries held out to their followers in contrast to the old religions, was the principal cause for their popularity. In addition to this hope, however, they appealed to popular taste for excitement by their secret rites and elaborate preparations for initiation. Household slaves brought them to the homes and nurseries of Rome, soldiers and merchants made them current in the market place. Isis, the Egyptian goddess who brought back her husband, Osiris, from the dead, and Cybele or Magna Mater from Asia Minor were the deities of two flourishing Mysteries. The Orphic cult centered around the Greek hero Orpheus who had in the legend gone to Hades, the abode of the dead, to restore to life his lover, Eurydice. Devotees of this latter cult were almost entirely women. The Persian hero-god Mithras, ally of the Sun against evil, was the only one who made any particular demands on the morality of his initiates. Soldiers were drawn to this mystery because of the strict discipline apparently (*cf.* Kipling's *A Song to Mithras*). Sunday was the holy day in Mithraism, a sacramental meal was the principal rite for initiates, and the members bound themselves in a brotherhood. It had one great shortcoming however; it was founded on a legend. It was easily Christianity's strongest rival in the Græco-Roman world, as it was most like Christianity of all the Mysteries. But its appeal was limited to men, and it lacked power to inspire its followers to suffer and die, if need be, in loyalty to the legend.

The Jews were another important religious element in the Empire in the first century of the Christian era. They had been scattered over the Roman world for two hundred years in what they always spoke of as the Dispersion. At times they were persecuted in one place or another (*cf.* for example Acts 18:2), but usually they were accepted and were happy enough. Two and a half centuries before Christ the Jews in Alexandria made a Greek version of their Hebrew Scriptures called the Septuagint, and by it Greeks were introduced to Judaism. The synagogue, which was the place of meeting for prayer and for instruction, church and school that is, throughout the dispersion was another means of propagating Judaism. Many Gentiles who were unhappy over the stagnation of their own religion were attracted to the two fundamental ideas of Judaism, belief in one God and insistence on morality among His followers. Some became proselytes or Jews by adoption; many more attached themselves to the synagogue without becoming full Jews, as did Cornelius whom Peter baptized (Acts 10), or the man of whom it was said in St. Luke's Gospel, "he loves our nation and has built us a synagogue" (Luke 7:5).

Stoicism was another force which, though not strictly religious, prepared men's minds for the Christian emphasis on morality. Duty and self-control were the highest Stoic virtues; sentiment had no place in the truly good man who guarded equally against laughter and tears. Any thought of reward was repugnant; "Virtue is its own reward." There was considerable talk of brotherhood, but it was held as an intellectual ideal more than as a principle of everyday action. The word "God" stood for "Law," as we speak of the laws of nature, meaning the principles we have discovered as prevailing in nature. Stoicism appealed to thinkers and philosophers as a system of high morality; and in Marcus Aurelius the Emperor, or in Epictetus the Greek slave, it was admirable though austere and unimpassioned. Yet it could not appeal to the ordinary man who loved his family and was concerned with their welfare, who rejoiced at homely pleasures and wept at the sorrows that came to him.

It is always possible to exaggerate the moral degradation prevalent in the Empire, but St. Paul was not indulging in rhetoric when several times he flashed out a warning to his converts against low standards of living that they had but lately escaped from (*cf.* Romans 1:24–32, Galatians 5:19–21, Ephesians 4:17–19, 5:3–12). Pagan writers are full of such references, and not merely those who retail the corruptions and scandals of court life. Oriental luxuries and the accompanying vices had flooded into the West after the time of Alexander the Great, and religion in general, as we have seen, offered little to counteract these influences. Some of the Mysteries appear to have encouraged immoralities, and neither Judaism nor Stoicism offered a widely accepted antidote to the prevailing degradation.

The causes for the low standards of morality are to be found in the foundations of pagan society itself. The institution of slavery was fundamental to its existence. Few people questioned its right to exist. Plato, one of the noblest thinkers of Greece, built his ideal state on this basis (*cf. The Laws*). It has been estimated that at the beginning of the Christian era there were half a million slaves in the city of Rome, one out of every three men seen in the streets was a slave. These slaves had rights in law that were often ignored in fact. They were frequently the superiors of their masters in intellect and even in character; the schoolmasters of Greece and Rome were slaves. When they lacked a conscience or had become embittered by their lot, they could take their revenge in the things they taught their masters' children, the vices they pandered to, the softness they encouraged.

As basic as slavery to pagan society was the low idea of

women that was found in Greece and Rome. Generally
speaking, women were little better than slaves. True, the
Roman matron was in higher standing than the Greek, just
as the native Roman virtues were superior to the Greek
virtues, but she was rarely the companion, intellectually or
spiritually, of her husband. She was in every way subject
to his wishes and authority. Paul reflects this view of
the relationship of husband and wife (I Corinthians
11:13-15, 14:34-35, Ephesians 5:22-23, Colossians 3:18-
19) and he was but saying what any man of his time
would say. The pious Jewish male thanked God every
day that he was not born a woman. It was this same Paul,
however, who, in an inspired moment, could write "There
is neither Jew nor Greek, there is neither slave nor free,
there is neither male nor female. You are all one in
Christ Jesus" (Galatians 3:28). To neither Jew nor Greek
did this make sense, and as for slaves and women it was
the dream of an enthusiast, a dream they did not even
dare to ponder.

Both slavery and a low regard for women are themselves based on a low valuation of men as men. If the
Pharisees in the Gospels had answered Christ's question
"How much more valuable is a man than a sheep?" they
probably would have said "That depends on who the man
is." The Roman would have answered in the same manner. That attitude is well attested in the gladiatorial shows.
Spectacles in the amphitheatres were used almost always
by the Emperor or the local governors to buy the favor
of the populace. Slaves and criminals were encouraged to
fight until they had cut each other to pieces. Only such
bloody spectacles amused the Roman people in the latter
days of the Empire. Another widely prevalent practice

was the exposure of unwanted babies. Parents seemingly felt no particular emotion at leaving their babies where they would be eaten by wild beasts. A recently discovered letter, bearing every sign of being authentic, from an Alexandrian merchant to his wife puts it plainly, "If our expected child is a girl put it out for the crocodiles to eat." There were thinkers who deplored such practices, but the accepted code of conduct demanded little. Into this situation came Christianity with its unheard-of demands and impossible standards, and to even the lowest in the social and moral scale it gave power to meet the demands. How this happened men could not say, that it did happen they could not deny. Herein lay the secret of Christianity's triumph in that decadent world. It met the moral needs of men, and this was in part what Christians meant by Redemption.

Not only in the moral sphere but also in the religious did Christianity give satisfaction to men's cravings. The many religions with their devotees in the Empire of the first century indicated that men were hungry for a religion that would satisfy. Christianity came with answers to these needs, and that was true, Christians said, because Christianity was God's act, God's response to man's long felt needs. They were convinced that Jesus brought men closer to God because in some way He was the Son of God, sent by God into human life for that purpose. Jesus was God in human terms, and He was no legend or pious fable. He was a fact in history. The Gospel of St. Luke was careful to give dates that could be verified, "the fifteenth year of Tiberius" (Luke 3:1), and the creeds gave the name of the Roman governor who put Christ to death.

Moreover when Christ had been taken away from the

sight of men, the Spirit of God, God's continuous presence, had made Himself known to Christ's followers, and the Church had been born. The Church, too, was God's act, God's response to man's continuing needs. It was no man-made organization, no group of like-minded people who felt that their ideals could be realized best by organizing a society. It was in a real if mystical sense "the Body of Christ," as St. Paul called it; and Christians were "members" of His Body, His means of living and working in the world, the "extension of the Incarnation." By the Church men were brought into a holy fellowship, a true brotherhood. Their needs were met, and their fellowship with God and with each other strengthened by the sacraments, His appointed means of grace and communion. Christians needed no password to attain immortality, they were already partakers of eternal life in the midst of time. They saw human life as the field of God's endeavor, and themselves as His means of restoring all men to their lost heritage as "sons of God and heirs of eternal life." The Christian faith triumphed in the Roman world largely because it had what science calls survival value, or as we have said because it met men's moral and religious needs.

Chapter 4

"THE NOBLE ARMY OF MARTYRS"

WHEN CHRISTIANS first appeared in Greece and Rome no one in authority thought of forbidding them their religion, much less of persecuting them. The answer of Gallio, the Roman proconsul in Corinth, to the Jews who tried to have him condemn St. Paul, was typical of the Empire's attitude, "I refuse to have anything to do with religious quarrels" (*cf.* Acts 18:12–17). Paul always thought of Rome as his protector; she saved his life from the mob in Jerusalem, and if finally he was executed along with other Christians by Nero, the mad Emperor, it was not the result of religious persecution. Nero was generally believed to be himself responsible for the fire that had destroyed the greater part of the city of Rome, and he had to find a scapegoat on whom he could fasten the blame. Christians were numerous enough and apparently unpopular enough by 64 A.D. for that purpose, so the Roman historian Tacitus tells us. "To stifle the report (*i.e.*, that he had started the fire) Nero fastened the guilt and inflicted the most exquisite tortures on a class hated for their abominations. The populace called them Christians . . . a vast multitude was convicted not so much of arson as of hating the human race."[1] Nero could appeal to a popular

[1] *Annals* of Tacitus, XV, 44.

prejudice already formed; and, according to long accepted tradition, both Peter and Paul perished in this outburst of hatred as well as many other Christians.

It is not easy to understand why such violent prejudice should have arisen so quickly, but several causes for unpopularity may be given. For one thing Christians had ceased to attend the games and other spectacles in the amphitheatre both because of their cruelties and because they were begun with prayers to the pagan gods. Moreover they had withdrawn from certain trades and occupations, particularly those that were connected with the old religions and those that were antisocial and nonproductive, among which were classed the making of jewelry and amulets, teaching horse racing, being a soldier as well as catering to the current immoralities. Hence Christians were considered to be disrupters both of business and of society. They were overscrupulous in these matters perhaps, but they knew from first-hand experience, as Paul had pointed out in his letters, how easy it would be for Christianity to fall back to the level of the Mysteries with no higher moral standards. Another cause for unpopularity and suspicion lay in the necessity for holding meetings at night. It is a fact that many of the first Christians were slaves or members of the working classes (*cf.* I Corinthians 1:26), who could meet only after the work of the day was done. But meetings at night and often in secret gave rise to charges of the darkest immoralities, though those who levelled the charge might indulge freely and openly in such practices themselves. The first Epistle of St. Peter in the New Testament referred to such charges (*cf.* I Peter 2:12–17, 3:14–17, 4:12–16), and tried to prepare Christians for violence as a result of them. Again since Christians had no image of their deity and refused to worship the old gods, they came to be called Atheists, people who had no god at all. Every public calamity then could be attributed to the anger of the gods at such impiety. A century after Nero the Christian writer Tertullian could say, "If the Tiber rises in flood or if the Nile does not rise, if there is an earthquake or famine or pestilence, the cry is 'The Christians to the lions.' " The other popular cry was "Away with the Atheists." The Roman Empire, however, like the proconsul Gallio in Corinth, was "concerned about none of these things."

Local persecutions, stirred up by officials for their own reasons or as mere outbreaks of popular passion, continued intermittently for some years. Then around the end of the first century of the Christian era the Empire found itself forced to change its policy. Though it had not cared what religion a man practiced it had demanded as a gesture of loyalty that every man sacrifice before the statue of the Emperor. Christians refused to do this because it seemed to compromise their stand against idolatry. Moreover they were said to speak much in their secret meetings about a "Kingdom of God." This had the ring of sedition in it. Rome became so nervous about sedition that the Emperor Trajan in a letter to Pliny the Younger, who was then governor of the province of Bithynia in Asia Minor, forbade the formation of a fire brigade for fear it might become a secret group, plotting rebellion.

The correspondence between Trajan and Pliny in the years 112 to 114 A.D. reveals the growing dilemma Roman officials faced because of the Christians. Pliny wrote to the Emperor that he had found the trade in animals for sacrifice ruined because the pagan shrines were deserted, and the cause for the desertion seemed to be the persuasiveness of Christians in winning men to their religion. Pliny ordered them to cease such practices and to sacrifice to the Emperor. Those who refused he put to death. Accusations were then made in wholesale fashion, and since informers shared in the estate of the man executed on such a charge Pliny began to suspect the accusations. Some men were willing to give up their faith and "curse Christ," but even those who remained steadfast did not seem especially dangerous. They met at dawn to sing a hymn "to Christ as to a god," and bound themselves by a soldier's oath of loyalty (as Pliny would understand the word *sacramentum*, though for Christians it may already have had some of the meaning of the modern word) "not to lie or commit fornication or steal." Later in the day these Christians met again for a meal together, a meal of fellowship (the *Agape* of I Corinthians 11). Pliny wrote Trajan for instructions as to how to proceed next. The Emperor replied in a dignified manner, but definitely, that it was a crime to be a Christian: "Christians are not to be hunted out, but if they are brought to you and the offense is proved they are to be punished, with this reservation, that if any one denies that he is one and makes it clear that he is not by offering prayers to our deities then he is to be pardoned." Persecution of Christians thus became a state policy.

The Revelation of St. John the Divine, or the Apocalypse, the last book of the New Testament, is the product of one of the periods of official persecution, most likely the attempt by the Emperor Domitian to enforce Cæsar worship in Asia Minor in 95 A.D. Apocalyptic is a style of writing, employed by the Jews in the book of Daniel, for example, which we may describe for the present purpose as cryptic. None but the initiated can understand. The purpose of the Revelation was to encourage those who suffered persecution. The final triumph of Christ is near at hand when "God shall wipe away all tears," but before that must come the last great trial which is referred to as the appearance of Anti-Christ (*cf.* chapters 12–14). A popular legend that Nero would come to life again seems to be the reference in the "beast that arises from the depths" (11:7), and the mysterious "number or cipher of the beast" which is "the number of a man, and his number is six hundred and sixty-six" (13:18) can be worked out to yield "Nero Cæsar." Those who "would not worship the image of the beast" clearly are Christians who would not sacrifice before the Emperor's statue. But reading this without the key, who could possibly understand? And who likewise would see in the last two chapters, in the coming of the "new Jerusalem," a vindication of the Christians and the reward of their faithfulness? In artistic terms the book is a great mural painting, on a large scale and in vivid colors, which can only be understood in the context of the persecutions of Christians by the Roman Empire.[1]

[1]*Cf.* E. F. Scott, *The Book of Revelation*, pp. 175–177 for the present day relevance of the book.

"At the present day, more clearly than ever before, we can read the message of John as if it were spoken directly to ourselves. By one of those strange reversions which sometimes come about in history, the situation for which the book was written has repeated itself almost to

Two great waves of Empire-wide persecution finally swept the Church, both of them savage attempts to destroy it entirely. The first came shortly after the year 250 when the Empire was preparing to celebrate the one thousandth anniversary of the founding of the city of Rome. Men looked back naturally to good old days and ways, and saw in the calamities of recent years the disfavor of the old gods. Christians seemed the centers of disloyalty, and the edicts issued against them singled out in particular the bishops as the leaders. Many perished, and many also relapsed into paganism or tried to compromise by securing from friendly officials papers which affirmed that they had sacrificed before the Emperor's statue. These were the *libelli*, whence our word libel. Finally the persecution died and the Church had peace for fifty years. Then came the last and fiercest attempt to destroy the new faith. The Emperor Diocletian, who promoted this persecution with such fury, was trying desperately to save the Empire from distintegration. Church buildings were burned and a thorough attempt made to find and destroy all copies of the Sacred Scripture of the Christians.

For nearly two hundred years Christians had had what we call the New Testament. The earliest Christian literature consisted of the letters of Paul, though they had been

the letter. It was taken for granted, not so many years ago, that this was quite impossible. . . . There could never again be a time when Christianity would be persecuted, when the State would declare itself the highest good, when human beings would lay claim to divine honours, when the very existence of a moral order would be denied. . . . But they have all come back. . . ."

"The truth is that Rome, as John conceived it, was only the type of what civilization must always be when it is divorced from any spiritual ends."

written, as we saw, with no thought of creating a body of sacred writings. Also the first disciples had made a collection of texts from the Old Testament which referred to Christ or were thought to have been fulfilled in Him. Next came the Gospels as we know them, written down from the recollections of eyewitnesses of Christ's life and certain collections of His sayings, written by men who had read and knew Paul's letters. Mark is the earliest of the four in the New Testament, but Luke in his preface clearly states that there were more than four. Several of these so-called "Gospels," attributed to Peter or to other New Testament names, still exist, and are usually spoken of as "Apocryphal Gospels," or sometimes as "lost" Gospels though they were never lost. We can understand, from their pitiful attempts to magnify Jesus by enlarging on the miraculous, why they were rejected by the early Christians. An interesting survival of some oral or written tradition, now lost, is to be found in the book of Acts where Paul says, "Remember the words of the Lord Jesus . . . It is more blessed to give than to receive" (Acts 20:35). We have no other record of that saying. The Acts of the Apostles set out to be a history of the earliest Christian community, especially of Peter and Paul, and is generally conceded to be the work of Luke who wrote the Gospel of that name. Both books are dedicated in their opening sentences to the same person who may have been a literary patron. Luke seems to have been one of Paul's companions on part of the missionary journeys, and to have incorporated his travel diary in the text of Acts in several places without taking the trouble to change the first person in which it was written (*e.g.*, Acts 16:10–17; 20:5–21:18;

27:1–end of book). The epistles of Peter, James, John and Jude are called General or Catholic Epistles because they were written to Christians generally and not to any particular group; together with the Epistle to the Hebrews and the book of Revelation they make up the rest of the New Testament. At this body of writing the persecution of Diocletian was specifically aimed, and our scarcity of manuscripts earlier than the fourth or fifth centuries is evidence of the thoroughness and success of this endeavor. But the Emperor was no more successful than his predecessors in stamping out the faith.

One of the foremost of the early Christians to suffer death in the first Empire-wide persecution was Cyprian, bishop of Carthage. He had been a wealthy pagan with great influence in the life of the city when in the year 247 he became a Christian. Because he saw its power in the daily lives of its followers he was converted to Christianity, and he consecrated his life and his wealth to the service of Christ. Within two years, against his will but at the demand of the Christians he was made bishop. Two years more and persecution broke out. Cyprian decided that his chief duty was to guide his flock through the trials and therefore he fled from the city. From hiding, by letter and by messenger, he encouraged the faithful, and each morning at his prayers he remembered those who had given their lives for the faith. When the persecution abated he returned to Carthage only to run into a new danger. Plague swept the city and countryside, and people fled in terror. Cyprian organized Christians into nursing and relief corps, and they cared for the sick, buried the dead and otherwise served without regard for the faith of those they tended. No sooner had the plague ceased than persecution broke out anew. Cyprian was exiled, and, as before, he guided his people from exile with special care for the clergy, many of whom were at forced labor in the mines. At the end of the year 257 a decree from Rome ordered death for the clergy and Cyprian returned at once to Carthage. The governor of the province was ill in another city and he sent for Cyprian to come and be judged there. Cyprian refused, having determined to die among his flock. Men begged him to flee but he would not. Finally on the 14th of September the governor was able to conduct the trial in Carthage, the whole city, Christian and pagan alike, being present. At the sentence of death the bishop answered *Laus Deo*, words with which he always ended his daily prayers. His death was a triumph, and from it came new life to the Church in Carthage and all North Africa. Truly, as an early Christian said, "the blood of the martyrs was seed" from which more Christians sprang.

In the years of persecution even in periods of peace, the only way for the Church to maintain a legal existence was to organize and register as a burial club. Hence it may well be called the Church in the Catacombs or burial places. Meetings must be in secret and informers waited to betray any one seen attending a Christian service. Secret signs and passwords came into use therefore, words with a secret connotation, some of them obvious enough to us such as the word used in Acts to describe Christianity, the *Way*, or such expressions as "a new name," "the cup of blessing," "the Good Shepherd." The sign most commonly used to direct Christians to a place of meeting was the drawing of a fish. Each letter of the Greek word for fish, *ichthus*, stood for another word, and the whole spelled a formula of the faith, a short creed:

I	esous	(Jesus)
CH	ristos	(Christ)
TH	eou	(God's)
U	ios	(Son)
S	oter	(Saviour)

Follow this sign as one follows arrows of direction and ultimately it led to a company of men and women professing this faith.

Membership in such a company was not made easy, however. A candidate would be taught the moral requirements of the faith and something of the Christian gospel, and a close watch would be kept that he had foresworn pagan ways. He became a *Catechumen* (whence the word catechism) or learner. Before Easter or Whitsunday he was taught the creed and the words said at the consecration of the bread and wine in the Communion. Then on the night before the feast he professed his faith in public and was baptized by threefold immersion, if that was possible, and received the laying on of hands, or Confirmation, and was admitted to the "Sacred Mysteries of Christ's Body and Blood" on the day of the feast itself. Such a baptism is described in detail in the *Didache*, or Teaching of the Twelve Apostles, a book written in the last years of the first Christian century before the New Testament was completely formed. The name Whitsunday for Pentecost probably is derived from the white robes worn by the newly baptized.

In New Testament times an Apostle, if one was present, would preside over meetings and services of the

Church. To preside in their absence Paul and Barnabas "set apart, or ordained, elders in every church" in Asia Minor (Acts 14:23). The word elder is the Greek word *presbuteros* or presbyter. Once in Acts these presbyters are called *episcopoi* or overseers, usually translated bishops (Acts 20:17 and 28). The English word bishop is derived from the Greek *episcopos*, as priest is derived from *presbuteros*. Other officials mentioned in the New Testament were the *diakonoi* or deacons, literally servants; the seven appointed "to serve tables," that is, attend to the business end of things, especially the care of the poor (in Acts 6:1–6), are usually called deacons though the word is not there used. The letter to the Philippians was addressed by Paul to "all the saints," that is, members of the Church, and then especially to "the bishops and deacons" (1:1); and in the first letter to Timothy Paul set forth the kind of life that was to be expected of bishops and deacons (I Timothy 3). These references give no clear picture of what we call the ministry, and indeed none is to be found in the New Testament. Nor is one to be found for some years. It has been well said that "the Church goes into a tunnel around the years 75 to 80 A.D. and does not emerge until the year 160." At least we know next to nothing about the Church in these years.

After the year 160 A.D. or thereabouts, however, historians are in a different position. The Church emerges, for one thing, with a definitely developed ministry in three kinds or orders. The place of the Apostles as presiding officers and chief ministers had been taken by bishops. A writer in the year 160 drew up a list of the bishops of Rome from the time of Peter and Paul. Presbyters were in charge of local churches and in the cities they formed a council

for governing the Church under the presidency of the
bishop. The third order comprised the deacons whose chief
function was the care of the sick and poor, but who also
were assistants to the presbyters in the services of the
Church. This ministry was not so much *over* the Church
however as *in* the Church. It represented the people who
formed the community of the faithful, and the community
was itself a priestly body because it was the Body of
Christ, the great High Priest.

The life of the Church in the Catacombs was summed
up in its worship, especially in the service called, in the
Didache, the *Eucharist* or the Thanksgiving, and which
has been variously known as the Lord's Supper, the Holy
Communion, the Mass. In the catacombs the service, held
often in secret at the tomb of a martyr with few lights, was
simple and brief, but followed a definite pattern and soon a
fixed form of words. Two early Christian writers have left
a record of such services. Justin Martyr in the *Apology,*
or defense he wrote of Christian practices about the year
150, described a service which he said was held on Sunday.
The *Apostolic Tradition* of Hippolytus, written about the
year 210, gave the actual words of the service. There was
first a preliminary service for the catechumens, consisting
of readings from the Old Testament prophets, from the
Epistles of St. Paul, and from the Gospels, and ending with
a short instruction on the Christian faith and life. The
catechumens then withdrew.

The service for the faithful followed the outline of the
Gospel account of the Last Supper where Christ "took
bread, gave thanks, broke it and gave to the disciples."
The people brought bread and wine from their own homes
and gave them to the deacon who spread a cloth on the

altar and laid the offerings on it. Some of these offerings were to be used for the poor, and some reserved for use in the Communion. A man who was being disciplined for his sins was not allowed to make an offering because the offering stood for his daily life and work, and they could not be offered to God unless they were holy. At this moment quarrels among Christians were dealt with and settled by the bishop, and each exchanged the "kiss of peace" or reconciliation with his neighbor before the service continued. The presiding minister then began the Thanksgiving prayer in which was included the words "This is My Body broken for you, Take and eat; This is My Blood shed for you, Do this as a memorial." The bread was broken with the words "Holy things for the holy ones," and was distributed to the people with the cup for their Communions, and the service came to an end with a deacon's dismissal. Some of the consecrated bread and wine would be taken by a deacon to the sick and those prevented from attendance. When the service was over, men and women went quickly to their homes or work, careful to escape detection, but their life in the world showed the effect of their worship. There they had offered themselves, their work and daily life, to God, and had received in return His life and strength, His Body and Blood. Their life in the world must reflect their offering and their Communion, as it must find its inspiration and sustenance at the altar. It has been said that the Christians won the pagan world because they out-lived and out-died their pagan contemporaries (*cf.* T. R. Glover, *The Jesus of History*). They were able to do this because they kept their daily life in constant touch with their Master Christ.

Chapter 5

ATHANASIUS

"Athanasius contra mundum"

THE YEAR 313 A.D. brought a great change to the status of Christianity. Constantine the Great and his co-Emperor, Licinius, issued the Edict of Milan granting toleration to Christians and placing them on an equality with pagans in the Empire. The Edict did not suggest that Constantine, who was the moving force in its issuance, had become converted to Christianity. It simply said, "the open and free exercise of their religion is granted to all others as well as to Christians." Christians were saved from further persecution by it, however, and they were more than willing to accept the current story of the Emperor's conversion. Before the battle of Milvian Bridge, it was said, when Constantine was challenged by Maxentius, who was a strong upholder of the old paganism, there appeared in the sky over the Emperor's head a fiery cross and the legend *In hoc signo vinces*. Constantine won the battle and immediately adopted a new standard for his troops, a spear with a crosspiece at the top and the letters X P (*chi rho*), the first letters of the

Greek word *Christos*. He remained Pontifex Maximus of the old religion but he became patron of the new. Apparently it had become clear to him that Christianity was the one force that could unify his tottering Empire. Thus Christianity increasingly came into favor at the court and became in reality the official religion.

The effect of the Emperor's patronage was by no means wholly good. Acceptance of Christianity became the surest way to his favor, and the religion of many was little more than a veneer to cover ambition and intrigue. It was this type of Christianity against which Julian, known in history as the Apostate, revolted. On becoming Emperor in 361 he tried to restore a purified paganism, largely on the model of Mithraism. He failed, partly because paganism could not be purified, but also because the current of real Christianity was stronger than he estimated. The court did not mirror perfectly conditions at large, and Julian was not so astute as Constantine had been in realizing the actual strength of Christianity. He paid an unintentional tribute to Christians moreover when he commanded the priests of his attempted revival to imitate the lives of ordinary Christians, to try to live up to their standards. By the time of Theodosius (379–395) all citizens of the Empire were required to profess Christianity, and the Emperor became the defender of the Church and the suppressor of false teaching. Thus the Roman Empire became Christian.

In the realm of public morals the influence of the Church in the early years of toleration was considerable. The spectacles in the amphitheatres and the gladiatorial shows, for example, for a long time were a scandal, and all the great Christian teachers had warned Christians away from them. But the shows continued. Toward the beginning of the fifth century in Rome a more forceful step was taken. One day at the spectacle with the usual crowd present a certain Telemachus, a Christian priest, threw himself into the arena between two combatants and was killed. This action dramatized the protest to such an extent that the Emperor abolished the shows with popular approval. In Roman law changes were made also that showed the influence of Christianity, crucifixion was abolished as well as the branding of criminals and the use of torture in examining the accused. Constantine placed the freeing of slaves in the hands of the clergy, thereby allowing the Church to bring pressure for their release. A typical sentence of manumission showing the religious import of the act read, "For fear of Almighty God and for the cure of my own soul, I liberate thee." Christians were bringing their influence to bear on life and society in a way that has well been called one act in a great drama.

Inside the Church another drama was being enacted, a drama of the Faith. Begun in Alexandria in Egypt and transferred by Constantine to Nicæa, a little town near his new capital, this drama soon had the whole Empire for its setting. The chief actors were Arius, priest in charge of a fashionable church in Alexandria, and Athanasius, a deacon of no importance or position when the action started, but later to become chaplain and adviser to the Bishop of Alexandria, and later still to become bishop himself. The drama began when Arius made statements about Christ which the bishop could not allow to pass unchallenged. Arius had the idea, typical of much Greek thought, that

God was so great and so holy that He of necessity was far removed from the world, and could never come into any intimate contact with men. Therefore Christ could not be the Son of God in any but a figurative sense. Arius did not say that Jesus was a man. Jesus was in a class by Himself, a semi-divine Mediator between God and man who took a human body, but not a human personality. Arius went further; he said it was still proper to worship the demigod Jesus, and thus he opened the way for a return of polytheism. Admit one demigod and the whole train might follow, Mithras, Æsculapius the Greek god of healing, and all the others.

When Arius was told that he must stop teaching this as the faith of the Church he replied by an appeal to the people in popular terms. He did not give lectures or ask men to judge on the merits of his views, he composed verses expressing what he had taught and set them to the popular songs and dance tunes of the day. He meant to set Alexandria singing, and then he doubted that any bishop could forbid his ideas. The songs caught the popular imagination. Every one sang them. Boatmen on the Nile rowed to the beat of "There was when He was not" or "The Son is subordinate to the Father." Merchants in the market place quoted their prices in Arian rhythm. Arius used the word Son to describe Christ, but he pointed out that a father always comes before his son in time and in place, and that was what Jesus meant by using the word Father. His logic was, of course, too logical; it made language describe completely a reality too great for language. He failed to see, as others have failed to see, that truth must always be expressed in a figure, even in a paradox, because truth is larger than human language and than human understanding. Arius wanted a short statement of the nature of Christ which his mind could grasp, and even more one which the minds of ordinary men could grasp. Then in case men still could not understand he called in music and rhythm and popular rhymes to help. The bishop was at a disadvantage.

Arius allowed himself to be misled by language in another particular also. St. Peter at Pentecost had called Jesus "both Lord and Christ" (Acts 2:36). The word *Lord* had a special meaning to a Jew. Whenever in the Scriptures the Hebrew name for God appeared the Jew never pronounced it, the sacred name could not be taken on human lips. He always substituted the word Lord, *Adhonai* in Hebrew. The Greek translation of the Old Testament, the Septuagint, substituted in the text the Greek word *Kurios*, Lord, which might be used (as in English) as a title or a term of respect, but which in the context was clearly equivalent to "God." The word *Kurios* however had religious connotations in Greek also, and this may have confused Arius. It had been used of Apollo in the old paganism, and it was taken over into Mithraism to describe the Persian divine hero. In this Greek context it meant a saving demigod or Saviour. To Arius, a Greek of the third century, these latter meanings may have been the important ones, but it was not so to the first Christians on whom the spread of the faith depended.

The first disciples whose background was Jewish knew nothing of any meaning of the word "Lord" save the Hebrew meaning. Yet they who had been brought up as strict believers in one God, and in Him alone, had least trouble in identifying the Jesus they had known with the God they worshipped. He with whom they had walked the hills and roads of Palestine, who "spake as never man spake" and who had died on the Cross and been raised again on the third day, had without doubt lifted them and other men near to God Himself. This they knew from experience. They had seen the "glory of God in the face of Jesus Christ" (II Corinthians 4:6). They understood that He could use the word Father to describe God because He was Himself in some way the Son of God, Son spelled with a capital letter. As Paul said to the Philippians: "Who (Christ) being by nature God . . . emptied Himself to take the nature of a servant and to be born as a man . . . and He humbled Himself in obedience to death, even the death of the cross. Therefore God has exalted Him and given Him a Name that is above every name, that at the Name of Jesus every knee should bow . . . and every tongue confess that Jesus Christ is Lord (*Adhonai, Kurios*) to the glory of God the Father" (Philippians 2:6–11).

When the writer of the Gospel according to St. John finished his narrative of the significant events in the life and work of Christ he added to it a preface or prologue in which he expressed the same faith in other terms, "In the beginning was the Word, and the Word was with God, and the Word was God. The same was in the beginning with God. All things were made by Him. . . . And the Word was made flesh, and dwelt among us, and we beheld His glory, glory as of the only begotten of the Father, full of grace and truth" (John 1:1–3, 14). The Apostolic faith clearly was that God had come to earth in the person of Jesus His Son; or, as St. John puts it elsewhere in the Gospel, "God so loved the world that He gave His only begotten Son" (John 3:16). This is what is meant by the Incarnation. This faith is what Arius, even if unconsciously at first, was denying, and thereby reducing Christianity to one of the Mysteries.

The Bishop of Alexandria was at another disadvantage in dealing with Arius. He had only his own authority and that of his Synod to appeal to. During the nearly three centuries of the Christian Church the faith had not been officially defined. There was no creed to which the whole Church gave assent. This fact does not mean that there were no creeds, it means there were many creeds. Each local church or district developed its own formula for use as a baptismal confession of faith. In the book of Acts there is a reference to such a confession (Acts 8:37). Philip, one of the Seven Deacons who was forced to leave Jerusalem after the stoning of Stephen, met an Ethiopian, or as we should say, Abyssinian official who was reading in the Hebrew Scriptures the passage about the Suffering Servant of the Lord (Isaiah 53). The official asked Philip to explain this passage, and naturally Philip "preached unto him Jesus," who for Christians had fulfilled the mission of the Servant. The Ethiopian then asked if he could be baptized into this faith and Philip replied that he could "if he believed with all his heart." The answer was "I believe that Jesus Christ is the Son of God." Even if this verse is a later addition to the narrative, as some scholars say (though it appears in one early manuscript), nevertheless it is obviously an early baptismal formula of faith. Out of such formulas came the creeds. The creed we call today the Apostles' Creed is a fully expanded baptismal formula whose origin is unknown except that it seems to have arisen in Spain or northern Italy shortly after the year 150. Although the Apostles' Creed can hardly have been composed by the Apostles, its elements are all to be found in the New Testament and it is a good summary of Apostolic teaching and preaching. The Church in the East had not used nor accepted this formula, however, as it has not to this day, and therefore the Bishop of Alexandria could not appeal to its authority.

The bishop saw clearly the danger in Arius' teaching, nevertheless, as did his young archdeacon Athanasius, and in 319 Arius was forbidden to preach. Arius had friends at court and in the Church, and Constantine, seeing the possibility that the newly recognized religion might itself become a center of dissension, ordered the quarrel to cease. But the theological field was one in which he could not command. As the quarrel grew in intensity Constantine sought for another solution. He summoned all the bishops of the Church to meet with him in Nicæa, near his new capital of Constantinople. The meeting was to be held in the summer of 325 A.D., the twentieth anniversary of the Emperor's accession to the throne. Imperial travel and posting facilities were put at the service of the bishops. They came, over three hundred of them, mostly from the East because the distance was too great for the Western bishops. Hosius of Cordova in Spain was the foremost Westerner to attend; the Bishop of Rome was represented by two priests, but they had no vote. Many of the bishops bore scars of torture and persecution, eyes gouged out, limbs crippled, hands missing. For them it was the hour of vindication. No longer were they the persecuted of the earth, they were the Emperor's chosen counsellors. Each bishop could bring two priests with him, and the Bishop of Alexandria naturally brought Athanasius as his chief adviser. Athanasius had no seat since he was not a bishop, but he soon became the leading figure at Nicæa.

Constantine's first act at the Council was to burn publicly all letters of complaint and recrimination which he had received from any of them and about any of them. Then, pleading with them to be as charitable toward each other, he opened the proceedings. Arius was called in to explain his position and after appealing to the logic of his views he broke into what he considered the best of his songs. Somehow episcopal ears and emotions were not susceptible to such an appeal. A statement drawn up by extreme Arians was presented to the Council but it was rejected. It was hardly an adequate statement of the faith for which they all had suffered and in behalf of which many known to them had died. Local creeds were offered and one from Cæsarea in Palestine met with considerable approval because it was drawn largely, though not entirely, from Scripture. When the Arians were prepared to accept this statement Athanasius became suspicious. Its words were indefinite and therefore susceptible of different, even contradictory, interpretations. Such a statement was what Arius desired. Athanasius began to look for a word or phrase that was not ambiguous. Some one quoted a letter written years before by a member of the Council in which it was said that Christ was "of the same *being* (or *essence*, in Latin *substantia*) with God." The Arians would not accept this word because it was definite and definitive. Athanasius became its champion. It is a better word in

Greek, the language of the Council and the resulting creed, than it is in Latin or English; *ousia* means "essential being," whereas *substantia* suggests something physical and material. Arius would have agreed to the phrase "of similar essence or being," but not to the one proposed. The difference between the two in Greek is that of one letter, and that letter the smallest, the *iota* or i. Hence arose the gibe about the "quarrel over an *iota*," but on such small things do great issues depend. Was Christ *homooussion*, "of the same essence" with God, or merely *homoioussion*, "of like essence?" The Emperor did not understand, neither did some of the bishops, but Athanasius made clear the dangers of the Arian phrase and won them to his position.

The Council finally agreed on a formula of the faith, which is the original of what is now called the Nicene Creed. It read in its first form as follows:

"We believe in one God, the Father Almighty,
Maker of all things both visible and invisible;
And in one Lord Jesus Christ, the Son of God,
Begotten of the Father, Only begotten,
That is, of the essential Being of the Father:
God from God, Light from Light, True God from True
    God,
Begotten, not made, Being of one essence with the Father;
Through whom (*i.e.*, Christ) all things both in heaven and
    earth are made;
Who for us men and for our salvation
Came down and was incarnate; and was made man;
Suffered and rose again the third day;
Ascended into the heavens;
Cometh to judge the quick (*i.e.*, living) and the dead.
And in the Holy Spirit."

As may be seen the Council was concerned only with the Person of Christ and His relation to God. Sometimes it is objected that the creeds do not deal with the facts of Christ's life, or with anything between His birth and death. These facts are to be found in the Gospels and are not, except for certain details in themselves unimportant, matters for dispute. The creeds are concerned only or primarily with essential facts of the faith that have been denied or called in question. Other Councils rounded out the clauses of this creed in the interest of more accurate definition, or in order to explain more fully what Christians believed about God the Spirit and His work in the Church. The Creed of Nicæa settled only one definition, but that was the one on which all the rest depend.

The quarrel, however, was in no wise settled by the Council's action. The followers of Arius still thought him in the right, and some of them accepted exile and deprivation of property and office rather than conform. On the other hand Athanasius, who became Bishop of Alexandria in 326, had a long and stormy experience trying to win over his opponents. When Constantine died his successors were not agreed as to the decision at Nicæa. Twice Athanasius was banished and his opponents put in control of the church in Alexandria. Once he was commanded to reinstate Arius without asking for his assent to the creed. He refused and was again banished. Imperial pressure turned many bishops Arian, and this gave rise to the saying *Athanasius contra mundum.* He was not afraid of being in a minority. Julian the Apostate recalled Athanasius in hopes of promoting the quarrel in the Church, but when Athanasius criticized his attempt to revive paganism he re-enacted the sentence of banishment. Athanasius found shelter with the monks in the desert of lower Egypt, and directed his work from exile. His enemies accused him of crimes and immoralities in hopes of discrediting him. Once they hid a bishop and accused Anthanasius of murdering him, bringing in as evidence a hand supposed to belong to the victim. At the trial in the midst of the defense a veiled figure was led into the courtroom. Athanasius asked to have the hand brought forth, and made his accusers swear that it belonged to the man he was said to have murdered; then he drew aside the veil and revealed the "murdered" man, alive and well and having two hands.

The people of Alexandria remained devoted to Athanasius through all these years. It was at their demand that he had been made bishop even though he had fled from the election. One of his returns from exile met with such response that one writer likened it to the triumphal entry of Christ into Jerusalem on the first Palm Sunday. When Julian the Apostate banished him the people wept and tried to hold him, but he smiled and said, "A passing cloud." It turned out so, for Julian died within a year and the bishop returned to Alexandria. During one exile the Emperor put a scoundrel, George of Cappadocia, in his place as bishop. The Arians adapted the legend of St. George and the dragon to the situation with Athanasius in the place of the dragon. But it was not George who won this time. He was murdered by one of his own suite, and shortly afterwards, one day Athanasius was discovered in the library of the bishop's house writing a letter and acting as if he had never been away. Once the boat with his pursuers in it nearly caught him, but his boatmen turned and rowed at full speed toward the pursuing boat. They were asked, as he lay hid in the bottom, "Is Athanasius far away?" "He is close by," they answered and rowed on. His last ten years were spent in peace in Alexandria building up the Church and the faith he had so valiantly spent his life defending.

Chapter 6

ST. AUGUSTINE

"Thou hast made us for Thyself, and our heart is restless until it rests in Thee"

As MIGHT HAVE BEEN foreseen the Christian faith was defined and formulated in the East where Greek speculation and philosophy were at home. The steps by which this formulation was achieved were compared to a great drama, the drama of the Christian creeds. In the West where men are more concerned with the practical affairs of life another drama was played, the drama of the Christian life, in which Christ who is the Son of God revealed Himself with power in the lives and hearts and minds of men. This drama, which is complementary to that of the faith, is to be seen in the life of St. Augustine of Hippo, who has himself told the story in his *Confessions,* one of the great classics of Christianity and the first autobiography in literature.

Augustine was born in 354 at Thagaste in North Africa, in modern Algiers. The ancient Punic language of Carthage was still spoken in the country districts, and racial feeling ran strong. His mother Monica was a Christian, but his father did not profess the faith, and Augustine was not himself baptized as a boy. He was sent to school to become a teacher of oratory and he early fell into evil ways.

"It was held up to me, as the whole duty of a boy, to obey those who exhorted me to get on in this world, and make a name in wordy arts . . . then was I sent to school to learn letters. Alas! I knew not what profit they were, and yet I was flogged if I was slow to learn. For this was the good old way. . . . I had no want, O Lord, of memory or capacity—these Thou gavest me in full measure for that age—but we loved play, and for this we were punished" (*Confessions of St. Augustine,* Book I, chap. 9).

"Even now I cannot understand why I hated Greek, which I was taught in my earliest school days. Because I loved Latin, the literature, I mean, not the grammar. But the first lessons of the Latin schools, reading, writing, arithmetic, I thought as dull and penal as Greek. . . . 'One and one make two,' 'two and two make four'; this was to me a hateful sing-song" (Book I, chap. 13).

"I even stole more than once from my father's cellar, and from his table, at the bidding of my greediness or that I might have something to give to other boys. . . . And in my play I often sought to get the mastery by cheating." (Book I, chap. 19).

"During that year [his sixteenth] were my studies interrupted. I was called home from Madaura, a neighboring city, in which I had lived to learn grammar and rhetoric. . . . I kept complete holiday in idleness enforced by straitened means and lived with my parents. The briars of unclean desires grew rank over my head and there was no hand to root them out. . . . With what companions I walked the streets . . . and wallowed in the mire" (Book II, chap. 3).

"Alone I should never have committed theft, wherein I sought not the thing stolen but the theft itself . . . [but] friends say 'Come let's do it' and we are ashamed not to be shameless" (Book II, chap. 9).

The next year he went to the rhetoric school or university at Carthage. He longed to join the fastest set there, but was held back by some inner compulsion.

"My studies . . . drew me to look towards the Law Courts and aspire to success at the bar. . . . Now I had reached the top of the school of rhetoric. . . . I would take no part at all in the wild doings of the 'Wreckers' . . . which was looked upon as the best set [the 'city fellows,' literally]. I lived among them feeling a kind of impudent shame, because I could not keep pace with them" (Book III, chap. 3).

He read a book by Cicero, a book now lost, called the *Hortensius:* "That book changed my mind, changed my very prayers to Thee, O Lord, and altered my purposes and aspirations" (Book III, chap. 5). As a result he was led to read the New Testament, something his mother had not been able to get him to do. But he was disappointed in its literary style: "They [the Scriptures] seemed unworthy to be compared with the stateliness of Tully [Cicero]" (Book III, chap. 5). The Latin version of the Bible in current use at the time was inferior from a literary point of view.

His father died, but his mother continued to urge him on with his ambition. He became interested in the teachings of a religious group called Manichæans, who based their teaching on a diluted Christianity, and an adaptation of Zoroastrian doctrine. They taught that men and women were not responsible for what they did, and hence that morality had no particular meaning. He continued to give some allegiance to this teaching for nine years, during which he said he was "misled and misleader," but he never really accepted Manichæism. It served him as an excuse for the things in his life which troubled his conscience. As a teacher of rhetoric, first in Carthage, then at home in Thagaste, he had formed a union with a woman, who was his wife in all but name for fifteen years. He never married her, perhaps because she was considered his inferior socially. His mother seems not to have been worried so much by the connection as by the fear that Augustine might marry the woman. They had a son whom he called Adeodatus ["given by God"]. "In those years I had one . . . not in that which is called lawful marriage . . . yet one only, remaining faithful to her" (Book IV, chap. 2).

At that time an offer came to go to Rome to teach.

"I was persuaded to go to Rome, and teach there what I was teaching at Carthage. . . . I was not attracted to Rome by the richer fees nor the higher dignity my friends promised me (though these considerations affected my decision), but my chief and almost sole motive was that the students were said to be quieter there, and restrained by a severer discipline, so that they did not burst noisily into the class rooms of other teachers" (Book V, chap. 8).

The "Wreckers" were less desirable as pupils than they had seemed as companions. His mother did not want him to go to Rome, and came to Carthage to prevent his going. To elude her he told her he was going to see a friend aboard ship, whereas he already had his own luggage on board, and once on the ship sailed away himself.

Teaching in Rome had its troubles also.

"I began diligently to apply myself to the object which had brought me to Rome, the teaching of the art of rhetoric. And first I gathered at my home a little company of scholars, to whom and by whom I was beginning to be known, when lo I discovered that there were vexations at Rome from which I had been free in Africa. It was true, as appeared, that young profligates did not practice 'wrecking' here, but, 'all of a sudden' said my friends, 'a number of them will enter into a plot to escape paying their fees, and march off to another teacher,' breaking their faith and despising justice for love of money" (Book V, chap. 12).

"When the Milanese sent to Rome, requesting the prefect of the city to provide them with a teacher of rhetoric . . . I made application . . . desiring . . . that upon due examination I might have the post. So I came to Milan where I found the bishop Ambrose. . . . I began to love him, not at first as a teacher of truth, which I despaired of finding in Thy Church, but as a fellow creature who was kind to me.

"Though I cared not to understand what he said, but only to hear how he said it . . . yet with the phrases which I loved, the facts which I had neglected began to trickle into my mind, because I could not keep them apart . . . first of all I began to perceive that what he said could be defended . . . especially after I heard one difficulty after another in the ancient Scripture explained. . . . I resolved therefore to be a catechumen [a learner] in the Catholic Church" (Book V, chap. 14).

"By this time my mother had come to me . . . following me over land and sea" (Book VI, chap. 1).

Augustine would have called himself a Neo-Platonist at this time, that is, he followed an adaptation of the teaching of Plato, the Greek philosopher. Many men of the time who felt that they could not accept Christianity on intellectual grounds were attracted to this philosophy. What it did for Augustine was to restore his faith in a man's ability to find the truth. Manichæism had made him

a sceptic, uncertain of anything, even that he was capable
of knowing the truth. Neo-Platonism, which has been called
"the culmination of all the idealism of Greece," convinced
him that it was possible for a man to discover enough truth
to live by. Yet it was not Augustine's intellectual hesitancy
that gave him the sharpest struggle. Though, as he said,
"the honorable name of marriage" was not given to the
union with his son's mother, yet seemingly he loved her.
Monica, however, wanting him to marry one of his own
station, persuaded him to send away the woman who had
been his wife in fact. This led to a worse situation.

"I was being urgently pressed to marry . . . already
I was a suitor, already a bride was promised, and none was
so eager as my mother . . . proposals were made for a
girl who was yet about two years too young to marry. . . .
I agreed to wait" (Book VI, chap. 13).

"Meantime . . . my mistress was torn from my side
as an obstacle to my marriage, and my heart, which clung
to her, was torn and wounded till it bled. She had gone
back to Africa, vowing unto Thee that she would never
know any other man, leaving with me my natural son by
her. But I, unhappy that I was, and weaker than a woman,
could not bear the delay of two years which must elapse
before I should marry my promised bride, and so, being
no lover of marriage so much as a slave to lust, I secured
another—I cannot call her wife . . . nor yet was the
wound healed which had been caused by cutting away my
former love" (Book VI, chap. 15).

Augustine's conscience was in revolt against his way
of life, especially after his mistress had been sent away and
he had taken another; but his will was not strong enough
to obey his conscience. He records at this time the oft

quoted prayer of his early manhood, "O Lord, make me pure . . . but not now."

"I knew for certain that it was better to yield to Thy love than to my lust, the love charmed but could not prevail, the lust pleased and bound me" (Book VIII, chap. 5).

One day he had been reading Paul's Epistle to the Romans, and the book was on his table when a visitor came to see him. In the seventh chapter Paul was not talking of Augustine's particular difficulty, but Augustine could not fail to see the appropriateness of Paul's words to himself.—"What I hate that I do. . . . To will is present with me, but to do that which is good is not . . . the evil which I would not, that I do . . . with my mind I serve the law of God, but with the flesh the law of sin" (Romans 7:15–25). The visitor who came at this time brought the struggle to a climax. He noticed the book on the table and expressed pleasure at it, for he was a professing Christian. Then he began to tell Augustine and Alypius, Augustine's companion, about St. Anthony in Egypt who to conquer lust had fled society and gone into the desert. There he had found as great temptations, but in the power of Christ had conquered them. When the visitor was gone, Augustine was in great distress.

"Disordered in look and mind by this desperate wrestle with my own soul . . . I fell upon Alypius crying out, 'What has come—what means this tale that we have heard? Simple men arise and take heaven by force, and we with all our learning wallow here in flesh and blood. . . . Shall we not follow if we cannot lead?' I scarcely knew what I said, and flung myself away, leaving him staring in silent astonishment . . . there was a garden to our lodging . . . thither the tumult of my breast drove me, where no one could interrupt the duel into which I had entered with myself" (Book VIII, chap. 10).

"I kept saying within myself, 'Let it be now, let it be now,' and as I spoke the word I was on the point of resolution. I was on the point of action, yet acted not. . . . Alypius kept close to my side and waited in silence to see the cause of my agitation" (Book VIII, chap. 11).

"There arose a whirlwind, bringing a violent burst of tears. I rose and left Alypius, till my weeping and crying should be spent. For solitude seemed fitter for tears . . . he guessed my feelings . . . [and] remained upon the bench to wait. I flung myself down under a fig tree and gave my tears free course . . . weeping in bitter contrition. . . . I heard a voice from the neighboring house, it seemed as if some boy or girl, I knew not which, was repeating in a kind of chant the words 'Take and read, take and read' . . . I began to think whether there was any kind of game in which children sang those words but I could not recollect that I had ever heard them. I stemmed the rush of tears and rose to my feet. I could not but think that it was a divine command to open the Bible and read the first passage I lighted upon. . . . I ran back to the place where Alypius was sitting, for when I quitted him I had left the volume of the Apostle lying there. I caught it up, opened it, and read in silence the passage on which my eyes first fell, 'Not in rioting and drunkenness, not in chambering and wantonness, not in strife and envying; but put ye on the Lord Jesus Christ, and make no provision for the flesh to fulfill the lusts thereof' (Romans 13:13–14)" (Book VIII, chap. 12).

This incident is usually spoken of as the "conversion" of Augustine. Obviously it was merely the crowning point of a process, which had begun in the reading of the *Hor-*

tensius, just as the Damascus road for Paul was but the high moment in a process. Augustine had never ceased to marvel that a man of the intellectual gifts of Ambrose, the Bishop of Milan, could be a Christian. Recently he heard from a friend of his that Victorinus, a great pagan teacher in Rome, had become a Christian. Victorinus had found that Christianity met his intellectual needs and could be accepted by a man of intelligence and culture. When Augustine heard this it resolved his doubts on that score. On top of that came the story of how Anthony had found in Christ redemption from his immoral desires, and this too was Augustine's need. In his garden in Milan he faced these two needs and also the solution that was offered him. His response came at once.

"I determined, as in Thy sight, to withdraw the service of my tongue . . . from the haunts of wordiness. . . . Fortunately but very few days remained before the holidays" (Book IX, chap. 2).

A friend lent him and his companions a country home at Cassiciacum.

"When shall I recall the whole history of that time of holiday? Nay, I have not forgotten it" (Book IX, chap. 4).

"As soon as the vintage recess was over, I sent word to the Milanese that they must find another dealer in words for their students. . . . And by letter I indicated to the sainted Ambrose, Thy bishop, my former errors and my present resolve, begging him to advise me which of thy books I should chiefly read to fit and prepare myself for the reception of so great a grace" (Book IX, chap. 5).

"When the time came for giving in my name we left the country and returned to Milan. Alypius also resolved to be born again in Thee at the same time. . . . We joined with ourselves the boy Adeodatus, my son after the flesh . . . Thou hadst made him nobly. He was but fifteen yet in ability surpassed many grave and learned men . . . we took him for our companion, as of the same age in grace with ourselves . . . and so we were baptized" (Book IX, chap. 6).

"We were considering in what place we could serve Thee most profitably, and were on our way back to Africa. But when we reached Ostia, the port of Tiber, my mother died" (Book IX, chap. 8).

There follows a long tribute to his mother and an account of their last conversation together, closing with these words:

"Then said my mother, 'My son, as for me, I find no further pleasure in life . . . there was but one object for which I desired to tarry a little longer in this life, that I might see thee a Christian before I died. My God has granted me this boon in full measure and running over . . . what do I here?'" (Book IX, chap. 10).

"Within five days . . . she was seized with a fever . . . we ran to her side . . . and [she] seeing my brother and myself standing by the bed asked us, 'Where was I?' . . . On the ninth day of her sickness, in the fifty-sixth year of her age, and the thirty-third of mine, that devout and godly soul was released from the body" (Book IX, chap. 11).

He returned to Africa after years of absence, and in Thagaste became as well known for his charity as for his learning and Christian character. His son's death at this time left him grief-stricken. He retired to the country with some friends to lead a quiet life of study and prayer, and to recover somewhat the use of his voice which had suffered from a throat infection. In 390 he journeyed to

Hippo, a town near Carthage, and was persuaded by the bishop there to seek ordination and become special preacher for the bishop. In the year 395 he was made bishop, associate to the old Valerius, whom he succeeded in the next year. Hippo was in an obscure African district, but Augustine spent the remaining thirty-five years of his life as bishop there. Among his duties he acted as civil judge, as did bishops generally. Beside this and the care of his flock he wrote letters in great abundance, many of which are preserved, and books and treatises that have profoundly affected Christian thought and history.

The *Confessions* is said to be more read in the original than any other Latin work save Virgil, and has been translated into nearly every civilized tongue. Begun in the year 398, twelve years after Augustine became a Christian, he gave as his reason for writing it that people were speaking too highly of him, when they little knew the truth of his life. Actually he wrote it to say to the world that he had had an experience of God that gave his life a purpose and a meaning, and he had to express his gratitude and his sense of dependence. The *Confessions* in reality was addressed to God, not to men. "Thou hast made us for Thyself and our heart is restless until it rests in Thee" he wrote in the first paragraph, and he meant he had found that rest, that peace of mind. Yet Augustine, like Paul, was aware that while he had been seeking he had also been sought, that while he had found God he had also been found by God. In a memorable passage he expresses this conviction. He is telling how he had deceived his mother and left Carthage for Rome.

"Thou didst deal with me in wonderful secret ways. . . .

Thou didst so deal with me then, that I was persuaded to go to Rome, and teach there what I was teaching in Carthage . . . why I departed hence and went thither Thou knewest, O my God; but Thou shewedst it neither to me nor to my mother. . . . She clasped me tight in her embrace, willing either to keep me back or to go with me: but I deceived her, and pretended that I had a friend whom I could not leave till the ship set sail. . . . She refused to go home without me, and I with difficulty persuaded her to pass the night in a chapel dedicated to the blessed Cyprian [the martyred bishop of Carthage] hard by the ship. But in that night I secretly set forth, and she remained to pray and weep. And what was she beseeching of Thee, O my God, but that Thou wouldest prevent me from sailing? But Thou, in Thy hidden wisdom, didst grant the substance of her desire, yet refuse the thing she prayed for, in order that Thou mightest accomplish in me what she was ever praying for . . . by my desires Thou wast drawing me to the place where I should bury my desires" (Book V, chap. 8).

He put the same thought succinctly elsewhere: *Teneo et teneor*—"I hold on and I am held on to."

Augustine's Latin style permanently influenced the language of the Church. He took a crisp and precise tongue and made it express the warm devotions of a man at prayer. No doubt his style grew out of his love for the classics, especially Virgil. He is said to have read or reread half a book of the *Æneid* every day. In the *De Civitate Dei* he quotes Virgil on nearly every page. There were others in his day who did not look so favorably on the old pagan classics, suspecting and deploring their effect on both the religion and the morals of the young. One of Augustine's contemporaries, St. Jerome, tells how, after he became a Christian, he clung to pagan literature being repelled, as Augustine had been, by the literary style of the Latin Bible. Once in a severe illness and near death, he had a vision of God's judgment of him. "I was caught up in spirit, and . . . before the judgment seat of God. When the voice asked me concerning my condition I replied that I was a Christian. 'Thou liest,' answered He that sat on the throne. 'Thou art a Ciceronian, not a Christian; for where thy treasure is, there will thy heart be also.' " On his recovery he foreswore the classics, and turned to making a literary version of the Bible into Latin, from the original Greek and Hebrew. This version, called the *Vulgate*, "in the tongue of the people" (*vulgus* in Latin), forms the official version, with revisions, of the Roman Catholic Church, and ranks in its effect on the language of the Church with Augustine's use of Latin.

Augustine lived at what may be called the end of one age and the beginning of another. When he was born in 354, the Empire to all appearances was secure, made so in part by the recognition granted the Christian Church. As he lay dying in 430, the Vandals had overrun Italy and were hammering at the gates of his little city of Hippo in North Africa. The barbarians were warriors and wanderers with little interest in a settled existence. They had neither intention nor desire to destroy the Empire. They were in search of food and security, but they were prepared to take it by force if necessary. Perhaps they also had something of the child's delight in destroying things, especially things that had no value in their eyes. When Roman officials first opposed them, and then fled before them, that was an invitation to pillage the towns of all they wanted. Roman gentlemen could no longer live in their country villas in peace, and pursue lives of leisure and the arts. Education had to give way to the strenuous life, and, except in the households of the bishops, no show of formal learning was maintained. Thus civilization came to a standstill. The barbarians struck fear into southern Europe and what remained of the Empire, and men said the old gods were having their revenge.

In this crisis Augustine wrote the *De Civitate Dei*, "Of the City of God." He maintained that the old gods had nothing to do with the prevailing political and social calamities. The clue to the fall of Rome was to be found in her failure to follow the admonition of his beloved Virgil, "To spare the conquered and strike down the proud." Back of human history stands God who demands righteousness and justice among men. Earthly kingdoms have frequently failed to achieve this, as Rome has failed, but the ideal remains in the minds of the most thoughtful citizens. This led Augustine to say that there is another kingdom or city than the "city of men" (*civitas terrena*), not so much of laws and boundaries as of spiritual kinship which binds together all those who love God and righteousness, both the living and the departed, angels and saints and men. This was the *Civitas Dei*, which was in reality a cross-section of all human history and all existing society, divine and human. It was the brotherhood of those who hold ideals of righteousness, and try to guide human institutions by them; perhaps some such word as citizenship would have served the purpose better. God had such a destiny for Rome if she had been willing to accept it, but she had not done so. Hence the calamity of the times had followed.

Augustine was picturing the ideal Christian state, whose citizenship transcended national boundaries, and whose ideals and purposes likewise were greater than those of any single state. In a sense it was a vision of the "new Jerusalem coming down out of heaven from God" (Revelation 21:2) and of the "city that hath foundations, whose builder and maker is God" (Hebrews 11:10). Yet it was no mere dream city, for Augustine felt that God would bring it into being on earth "for the healing of the nations." The Church was the earthly representative of the heavenly city, but not identical with it. Such a view was held by some churchmen, but was sharply disputed by earthly rulers. Both Charlemagne at the beginning of the ninth century, and the Emperors of the Holy Roman Empire in the tenth, consciously built their temporal realms on foundations which they understood the *De Civitate* had laid.

Augustine, though he was typical of the practical West, nevertheless profoundly influenced the thought and mind of Christians both in his own day and in the centuries since. He was a great theologian and all the more so because he worked out his theology in his life, or better from his life. As an example of this the most obvious is his teaching on sin and redemption. The *Confessions* made it abundantly clear that he had known them both, personally and intimately. He was never tempted to deny the reality of evil because he had experienced its power, not only in the world around him, but in his own life as well. Furthermore he knew that he had been saved from degradation not by his own efforts, however much he had tried; he had been saved by nothing but by God's overwhelming love and power, which he came to call "grace." He had not deserved it, nor had he expected it, but such was God's way. Of these facts he was certain and not particularly concerned to enter into controversy about them. But rival views which belittled God's grace and human sin, and saw men able by their own free will to rise above evil, were widely preached by the British teacher Pelagius. Augustine disputed such an easygoing optimism as not founded on the facts of human life. The steps in the argument need not concern us, both disputants accepted the historical character of the Garden of Eden, and of Adam and Eve. Augustine maintained that Adam's sin had entered into the race, that all the sons of Adam inherited the weakness as a moral disease and hence were by nature prone to sin. This is the doctrine of "original" sin, and Pelagius denied it. He held that men might be affected by Adam in that they might be drawn to imitate him, but in no other way. He even maintained that no evil a man might commit himself would affect him in the future, and each time the desire to sin arose, man was capable of turning it aside by his own power. To Augustine this was simply not true, as he knew by his own experience; he had desperately tried to avoid sin and found, as St. Paul had found, that he could not. It is his argument from experience, which gives his ideas such weight, added to the fact that so many men find themselves tragically in the same case. Only the free grace of God is sufficient to save men from their sins, and that grace is abundantly able to do so. Pelagius sounded so plausible, but he was in reality furnishing men with less than no hope—he was misleading them.

There were other less important strands to Augustine's thought, some of which have caused great distress in later days. Augustine felt that men actually inherited Adam's guilt as well as his weakness, and this idea was reflected in various forms of Calvinism and Puritanism. Augustine said that God chose those whom He finally saved by His grace, and this doctrine of predestination came to be interpreted as meaning that He capriciously chose some and not others. Throughout the discussion Augustine was reaffirming the fundamental unity of the race when he traced man's proneness to sin to a common ancestor. In a controversy with the Puritans of his day, called Donatists, who wanted to thrust every sinner out of the Church, Augustine maintained that if this were done none would remain inside, and moreover he made it clear that no small groups can assume the right to unchurch every one else. He was a churchman who saw the spiritual pride of the Donatists as deadly sin, and who felt that it was bound to lead to quarrels and divisions over the most sacred matters. For him the Church was the home of sinners, and their meeting place with God, not the society of the self-conscious saints.

In all this controversy, however, we must not miss Augustine the man. The charm of the *Confessions* lies in their humanity, in his boyish ambition to belong to the "gang" in Carthage, or his deep devotion to his mother. The secret of his enduring appeal can be found in his own words, "Life is kindled on life. One loving spirit sets another on fire."

Chapter 7

BENEDICT OF NURSIA

"Orare est laborare, laborare est orare"

FEW PEOPLE who have tried have found it easy to pray.
A great many "say their prayers" in the last few seconds
before they go to bed, fewer do something similar in the
morning. Truly to pray however takes effort and time
and perseverance, and people often object that they have
too many things to do. They have to choose between prayer
and work, and they choose work, admitting that prayer
is a fine thing to add to life when work is done, if there
is still time. To St. Benedict this would be a curiously
inverted way to look at things. All life to him was of a
piece. Part of it must be spent in the everyday tasks, the
work of the world, but part must also be spent preparing
for the work, and offering the work to God who is the
Master Workman. Work and prayer were the two important forms of activity, neither could be neglected, and
oftentimes it was impossible to draw the line between them.
He wrote over the door of his monastery chapel for all
the monks to see as they entered, "To pray is to work,"
saying in effect, "You are not leaving behind the useful
occupations for a period of quiet leisure, you are entering
on an activity that will take all your attention and energy,

and you are as surely accomplishing something as when you are elsewhere at work." Then for the monks to read as they left the chapel he wrote over the door, "To work is to pray," that is, "You are not leaving God behind when you leave the chapel, you are taking the same attitude and purpose out into the world that you had in the house of prayer, but you are being no more useful at work than you were at prayer."

The first criticism levelled against monks today is usually on the ground of usefulness. St. Benedict would not have been greatly bothered by it. In the falling Roman Empire the day for doing useful things seemed past. There was not very much to be accomplished by what men usually mean when they say "useful." In the year 476 the Empire in the West had come to an official close; the boy Emperor had been deposed by the West Gothic chieftain, Odoacer, and the regalia of office sent to Constantinople. The Eastern Emperor henceforth ruled Italy and the West by an official called the Exarch, and that official invariably retired to the security of the marshes around Ravenna whenever danger threatened. St. Benedict's earliest biographer, Pope Gregory the Great (*circa* 600), referring to the Lombard invasions that soon swept over Italy, wrote, "I know not what goeth on in other parts of the world, but in this land wherein we dwell the world doth not so much announce as visibly show its own last end." Benedict retired from the world in much the same state of mind; yet Benedict and Gregory were, paradoxically enough, among the world's most useful citizens. Complete destruction did not overtake civilization, and the saving force, though unintentional, was St. Benedict and the monasteries. Men fled from the world and by fleeing saved it; that is, they fled from its crudeness and rottenness, and founded retreats for peace and study and labor and prayer. The men of finest spirit and sensitiveness, of insight and genius even, were to be found not in the marauding bands of warriors, nor in the sinking structure of civil life, but in the monasteries. There were the artists, the poets, the students and scholars, the men of serious intent. They preserved learning and maintained the dignity of honest labor as against the false glory of warfare and corrupt politics, and in so doing saved European civilization from disintegration. They were able to do this because in the midst of disorder and anarchy they lived ordered and disciplined lives, and thus were able to cultivate the qualities in men that produce and preserve the civilized community. The man of today who sincerely questions the usefulness of monks would most likely in that day have been among the first to enter the monastic life.

Monks and monasticism had existed of course before Benedict. Very early in the East Christians began to practice hermit forms of asceticism as a protest against the failure of many so-called Christians to follow their Master's teaching strictly. But the life was wholly individualistic, often taking extreme forms of self-discipline. The classic example is Simon Stylites, who sat for years on a column, and was fed by those who thought him an unusually holy man for so doing. In Egypt countless men and women deserted the ordinary ways of life and went off into the desert to live alone because they felt that God could best be served away from the world. Perhaps the most weighty charge against them is that they were without social consciousness, they looked for conflict in the Christian life but forgot that the conflict might best be waged in behalf of others. Such asceticism did not appeal to men in Western Europe. Nor was it practical in a climate where the winters might be cold and food scarce. Community life was a necessity. If monasticism was to be acceptable in the West it must be adapted to the mind and conditions of Western life. The man who so adapted it was Benedict.

About the life of Benedict little is known. He was born in the year 480 in the town of Nursia among the Apennine mountains, in country of great beauty. His family was of noble blood and he was educated as fitted his station, though the barbarian invasions made his future uncertain. Gregory the Great, in his Life of Benedict, tells us that he was a serious youth. At the age of fifteen he went to Rome with his parents and sister to pursue his education, but he was ill at ease among city-bred companions. He missed the mountains and woods, and seems to have been repelled by the life of the city, which in the corruption and confusion of the times was not of very high quality. In a short time, a few years perhaps, he fled from the city into the foothills of the Abruzzi. His family seemed willing that he should stay, thinking it was a passing fancy, and he made his home in a cave near the ruins of one of Nero's villas. Here he was fed by a neighboring hermit who, the story goes, used to lower his food to him in a basket. The legend goes on to say that the monk used to ring a terra cotta bell, such as is still used in Italy for goat bells, to let Benedict know that his meal had come. The devil, observing this and anxious to remove Benedict from the scene, broke the bell by throwing a stone at it, and, unless his friend and provider on the cliffs above had discovered the loss, Benedict might have died of starvation, so intent was he on his devotions.

His fame grew until disciples flocked to him, and he formed them into companies of twelve each for mutual help and guidance. A body of monks from a neighboring valley persuaded him to become their superior. He hesitated because he doubted whether they would accept his ruling; and sure enough shortly after he had accepted, they tried to poison him. Benedict returned to his cave. Again he was drawn from his seclusion, this time by the noble friends of his family who wanted him to take over the education of their sons, and found what was virtually a school. A priest of the vicinity plotted to get rid of him, and Benedict finally made the move which was to influence the history of Western Europe.

What he had been seeking was more seclusion, and he found it in Mount Cassino, a steep hill, eighty-five miles southeast of Rome, rising abruptly out of a fertile valley, and fully as beautiful as his earlier retreat. He and his companions found there a deserted temple of Apollo, for it had been a sacred spot before, and this they rebuilt to serve as a chapel. Here in the year 529, which also marked the closing of the Pagan schools in Athens, he founded a monastery over which he presided until his death twelve or fifteen years later. He took the experience gained as hermit and schoolmaster and codified it in a Rule, "a very little rule for beginners" he called it, by which the life of the monastery should be governed. Compared with other earlier monastic regulations, or with the uncertain life of the world at that time, the Rule made demands of no great severity. It was marked by moderation and common sense. Its chief force lay not in regulations or in organization, but in the inner principle of being willing to submit to discipline for a purpose.

The abbot was to be a "father," which is what the word means, to the community, in which there were to be no distinctions of class or birth. Communism was fundamental to the life of the monastery.

"No one, without leave of the abbot, shall presume to give or receive or keep as his own anything whatever; neither book, nor tablets, nor pen; nothing at all. . . . All things are to be common to all, as it is written, 'Neither did anyone say or think that aught was his own.' Acts 4:32" (*The Rule of St. Benedict*, chap. XXXIII, "Ought Monks to Have Anything of Their Own?").

The details of living, sleeping, and eating are carefully thought out, and ordered, not without a touch of humor.

"If it be possible let them all sleep in a common dormitory. . . . Let a candle be constantly burning in the room until morning, and let the monks sleep clothed and girt with girdles or cords; but they are not to have knives at their sides in their beds, lest perchance they be injured whilst sleeping. In this way the monks shall always be ready to rise quickly when the signal is given and hasten each one to come before his brother to the Divine Office. . . . The younger brethren are not to have their beds next to each other, but among those of the elders. When they rise for the Divine Office let them gently encourage one another, because of the excuses made by those who are drowsy" (*The Rule,* chap. XXII, "How the Monks are to Sleep").

"We believe that it is enough to satisfy just requirements if in the daily meals, at both the sixth and ninth hours, there be at all seasons of the year two cooked dishes, so that he who cannot eat of the one may make his meal of the other . . . if there be any fruit or young vegetables [*i.e.,* lettuce, etc.] these may be added as a third dish. Let a pound weight of bread suffice for each day, whether there be one meal or two. . . . If, however, the community has been occupied in any great labor it shall be at the will, and in the power of the abbot, if he think fit, to increase the allowance so long as every care be taken to guard against excess, and that no monk be incapacitated by surfeiting. . . . All save the very weak and sick are to abstain wholly from eating the flesh of quadrupeds" (*The Rule,* chap. XXXIX, "Of the Amount of Food").

"The amount of other people's food cannot be determined without some misgiving. Still, having regard to the weak state of the sick, we think that a pint of wine a day is sufficient for any one. . . . Although we read that wine is not the drink of monks at all, yet, since in our days they cannot be persuaded of this, let us at least agree not to drink to satiety, but sparingly" (*The Rule,* chap. XL, "Of the Measure of Drink").

"Let clothing suitable to the locality and the temperature be given to the brethren, for in cold regions more is needed, and less in warm. . . . We believe, however, that in ordinary places it will be enough for each monk to have a cowl and a tunic; in winter the cowl being of thicker stuff, in summer of finer cloth. He should have a scapular for working purposes, and shoes and stockings for the feet. Monks shall not grumble at the color or coarseness of these things; they shall be such as can be procured in the districts where they live, or bought at the cheapest price. Let the abbot see to their dimensions, that they be not too short, but of proper length for those who use them. When receiving new clothes the monks shall always give back the old ones at the same time, to be put away in the clothes-room for the poor. For it is sufficient that a monk have two tunics and two cowls, as well as for night wear as for the convenience of washing. . . . Those who are sent on a journey shall get underwear from the wardrobe, which on their return, when washed, they shall restore. . . . A mattress, blanket, coverlet and pillow are to suffice for bedding" (*The Rule*, chap. LV, "Of the Clothes and Shoes for the Brethren").

"Let baths be granted to the sick as often as it shall be expedient, but to those in health . . . they shall seldom be permitted" (*The Rule*, chap. XXXVI, "Of the Sick Brethren").

"Any one on first coming to the religious [*i.e.*, monastic] life should not find the entrance made easy. . . . If, however, the newcomer continues to knock . . . and persist in his petition he shall then be allowed to enter the guest-house for a few days. After that let him be in the novitiate. . . . Let all the rigor and austerity of our journey to God be put clearly before him. If he promise to continue in steadfast perseverance, at the end of two months let the entire Rule be read to him. . . . If he still persevere . . . after the lapse of six months let the Rule be read to him again, that he may fully know the kind of life he is entering upon. If he yet persevere, after four months the Rule shall be read to him once more. If after due deliberation he shall then promise to keep all the law and do whatever is commanded of him, let him be received into the community" (*The Rule*, chap. LVIII, "The Manner of Receiving Brethren").

The purpose of the monastery may be described as threefold, (1) Worship, (2) Work, and (3) Study. Worship, which Benedict called the *Opus Dei*, was of first importance.

"Let the Oratory be what its name signifies [*i.e.*, a

place for prayer] and let nothing else be done or discussed there. When the 'work of God' is ended let all depart in strict silence . . . so that the brother who may wish to pray privately may not be hindered" (*The Rule*, chap. LII, "Concerning the Oratory").

The periods of daily corporate prayer, called "Hours," were seven in accordance with the Psalmist's custom, "Seven times a day do I praise thee" (Psalm 119:164).

"The sacred number of seven will be kept by us if we perform the duties of our service in the Hours of Lauds, Prime, Tierce, Sext, None, Evensong and Compline" (*The Rule*, chap. XVI, "How the Day Divine Office Is to Be Said").

Besides these there is a night service, or office, called Matins or Nocturns, which also goes back to the Psalms for its authority, "At midnight I will rise to give thee thanks" (Ps. 119:62).

"In the winter time—that is, from the first of November till Easter, the brethren shall get up at the eighth hour of the night by reasonable calculation, so that having rested till a little after midnight they may arise refreshed. Let the time that remains after Matins be used, by those brethren who need it, for the study of the Psalter or lessons. From Easter to aforesaid first of November let the hour for saying Matins be so arranged, that after a brief interval, during which the brethren may go forth for the necessities of nature, Lauds, which are to be said at daybreak, may presently follow" (*The Rule*, chap. VIII, "Of the Divine Office at Night Time").

The "hours" of the day and night were not equal in length since the period of daylight and the period of darkness were divided into twelve hours each. In the long days of summer an "hour" was about eighty minutes, in the winter the "hour" was about forty minutes. The "eighth hour of the night" in winter would be between half past two and three o'clock in the morning, but the monks had slept, supposedly, since five o'clock the afternoon before. Even here Benedict inserted a saving phrase, "by reasonable calculation." On Sunday a more elaborate schedule was followed, "let the brethren rise earlier," and minute directions were given as to the order of the service. Benedict showed his awareness of human weakness, however, in his provision for Sunday Matins.

"If any one shall come to Matins after the "Gloria" of the 94th Psalm [*i.e.*, the second Psalm of the Office] which on this account we wish to be said *slowly* and *leisurely*, he shall not take his place in the choir, but go last of all, or to some place apart. . . . We have judged it fitting that these should stand last, or in some place apart, in order that, being seen by all, for very shame they may amend. For if they remain outside . . . some one will, perhaps, return to sleep" (*The Rule*, chap. XLIII, "Of Those Who Come Late to the Divine Office").

It was ordered "that every week the whole Psalter of a hundred and fifty Psalms be sung" (*The Rule*, chap. XVIII). The arrangement of the Psalter by days of the month in the Book of Common Prayer is an adaptation of the monastic recitation of the Psalms, which is the backbone of the monastic offices or "Hours."

Furthermore, in line with Benedict's sense of the common good,

"All prayers made by the community in common . . . should be short" (*The Rule*, chap. XX).
"The brethren are not all to read or sing in course but only such as may edify the hearers" (*The Rule*, chap. XXXVIII).

The rest of the monk's day is to be spent in work and study, except that in summer a siesta was permitted after the noonday meal. Actually a monk slept eight and a half hours, worked with his hands six and a half hours, read and studied four, worshipped and prayed four, and had one hour for meals and intervals.

"Idleness is an enemy of the soul. Because this is so the brethren ought to be occupied at specified times in manual labor, and at other fixed hours in holy reading. . . . If . . . the nature of the place or poverty require them to labor at gathering in the harvest, let them not grieve at that, for then are they truly monks when they live by the labor of their hands. . . . Let everything, however, be done with moderation for the sake of the fainthearted. . . . During the Lenten days let each one have some book from the library which he shall read through carefully. These books are to be given out at the beginning of Lent. It is of much import that one or two seniors be appointed to go about the monastery at such time as the brethren are free to read, in order to see that no one is slothful, given to idleness or foolish talking instead of reading, and so not only makes no profit himself but also distracts others. . . . If, however, any one be so negligent and slothful as to be unwilling or unable to read or meditate, he must have some work given him" (*The Rule*, chap. XLVIII, "Of Daily Manual Labor").

"The brethren are so to serve each other that no one be excused from the work of the kitchen unless on the score of health, or because he is occupied in some matter of great utility. . . . On Saturday, he who ends his weekly service must clean up everything" (*The Rule*, chap. XXXV, "Of the Weekly Service in the Kitchen").

The Benedictine Rule created centers of prayer and

manual labor that were virtually self-supporting. The insistence on manual labor, on the duty of every member of the community to take his place in the field, produced a new point of view in society. In the Roman world for centuries only slaves had tilled the land, and the free man had considered farming beneath him. Here were men of birth and ability willing to dig and act as farm laborers. "Laborare est orare" takes on new meaning when this provision of the Rule is viewed in its historical setting. The requirements for reading and study, though they are scant in the Rule itself, made it necessary for every house to have a library. This led to the copying of all the books that were available, the Latin classics forming the bulk of these. Men copied and recopied the manuscripts, competing with each other in the artistry of their work, and studying as they copied. The schoolmasters of the Middle Ages were all monks, as were the historians and chroniclers. Our sole source for the history of Christianity in England in the early days is the *Ecclesiastical History of the English Nation* by the monk Bede. The monasteries, built by the hands of the monks themselves, were also the homes of artisans and craftsmen of distinction.

The prime virtue of the monasteries was charity. They furnished the only asylums for the beaten in life's battles, and for the sick and the disabled in an age that had no means of caring for such. As Houses of Refuge they shielded many an innocent man from summary injustice, and for the penitent criminal they became permanent "penitentiaries," where he might make reparation and show his remorse in a new life of prayer and usefulness. Among themselves the monks tried to cultivate the human qualities, life in a monastery was comparable to life in a family. One of the virtues to be cultivated was *hilaritas*, which we weakly translate as "joy." Before all this, however, their chief purpose was religious. Whatever they did was done *Ad majorem gloriam Dei*. Their sense of obligation to others, their willingness to dig, their concern for learning and art were all subordinate to their consecration to religious living. This ideal kept them true to the other ideals, and such was St. Benedict's aim and vision.

The later history of monasticism has in it much that is glorious and much that is tragic. With the inevitable wealth that came to the monasteries came also corruption and degeneracy. In the year 910 at Clugny in France an attempt was made at reform. The Abbot of Clugny became the head of the first Order and the Superior of other Benedictine houses in France which had been, until this time, independent of each other. The centralized authority did not however make for a stricter discipline. In 1098 at Citeaux, near Dijon in France, the Cistercian Order came into being with a stricter Rule than Benedict's. Bernard of Clairvaux, who wrote the hymn, *Jesu, dulcis memoria,* "Jesus, the very thought of Thee," was head of this Order. Many of the largest and most powerful English monasteries were Cistercian houses, Fountains Abbey in Yorkshire and Tintern Abbey in the Wye Valley. The ruins of these monasteries reveal something of the glory of Gothic architecture as it was developed by the monks, and at the same time some of the wealth that led to the downfall of the communities. Cistercian monks introduced sheep raising into England and thereby were an important factor in the economic growth of the kingdom.

Around the year 1090 an attempt was made at Chartreuse, near Grenoble in the south of France, to return
to the hermit type of monasticism. Diet was limited and
hair shirts worn in order to mortify the flesh, but the new
Rule was never very popular. The English public school
Charterhouse is so called because it was originally founded
in the buildings of this order, Charterhouse being an English attempt to say Chartreuse. The chief work of the
monks in the West came to be the winning of the heathen
tribes in northern Europe to the Christian faith as we shall
see. After this great work was done, however, the monks
often tended to retreat within themselves and enjoy their
own life and accomplishments. They gained great riches
in land and gold, and with the riches came sloth and a
falling off of devotion both to their prayers and their
charities. Yet the corruption of the later monasteries does
not detract from the work of St. Benedict. He himself
would not have been surprised at it, for he recognized the
power of sin and the need for vigilance. It was not the
Rule, but the failure to keep the Rule that led to such
degradation. And the fact remains that it was the Benedictine Rule that saved European civilization in the Dark
Ages. Moreover, as Gregory the Great said, the Rule is a
mirror held up to the life of Benedict himself. "The man
of God, Benedict . . . wrote a Rule for monks, remarkable for discretion and rich in instruction. If any one desires to know more deeply the life and character of the
man, he may find in the ordinances of the Rule the exact
image of his whole manner of living: for the holy man
cannot possibly have taught otherwise than as he lived."
(*Dialogues of St. Gregory,* Book II, chap. XXXVI.)

Chapter 8

"SERVUS SERVORUM DEI"

THOUGH ST. BENEDICT built better than he could foresee, the monasteries founded on his Rule were not the only forces making for stability and order in the Dark Ages. A new power had already arisen in old Rome which became the ally of the monks as a conserving force. This was the Church and the bishop of the ancient capital. Throughout western Europe generally bishops found themselves forced to assume governmental responsibility. Civil officials had fled, civil machinery of administration had disappeared, and the bishops were the only educated men who remained at their posts. They were, by training in language and often in law, the inheritors of the traditions of the dead Empire. Their courts and schools were the only ones that functioned. Some of them doubtless entered the Church as the only field open for public service and administration, the gifts which so strongly marked the Roman character. While this was true of the bishop of any important town, the city of Rome offered a particular field of opportunity. Hence Lord Bryce wrote, "the true heir of the Roman Empire was the Roman Church."

The Roman people themselves had accepted the bishop as their ruler as a matter of course, when they saw him doing for them what civil rulers failed to do. In 452, for example, even before the weakling Emperors in the West disappeared, when Attila the Hun threatened to sack Rome, it was the bishop, Leo I, who saved the city, by force of personality, or by bribery, or both. Ordinary men did not care much about his method, but they gratefully accepted the result; and the bishop became the strong man whose ability and initiative saved them from the dreaded Hun. Though Leo failed to prevent the Vandals from sacking the city in 455, he was believed to have saved it from complete destruction, and the citizens from slavery.

A century and a half later this growing influence of the Bishop of Rome was united with the youthful vigor of the Benedictine Rule in the person of Gregory I, rightly called Gregory the Great. He was born of a patrician family which had frequently given men to the service of the State. He followed in that tradition, and in 573 became Prefect of the city of Rome, though the position was not an enviable one. The heathen Lombards, who were in control of northern Italy, were bent on enlarging their dominions. The Roman army, such as it was, had retreated along with the Imperial officials to the marshy security of Ravenna. Gregory's own description of the times gives no hopeful picture: "Sights and sounds of war meet us on every side. Cities are destroyed, the land devastated, the earth depopulated. No one remains in the country, scarcely any inhabitants in the towns. . . . Before our eyes some are carried away captive, some mutilated, some murdered." In his post as Prefect he came to see no way out of the chaos except the way of St. Benedict. He therefore turned over a house in Rome to the Benedictine community which had been driven away from Monte Cassino by the Lombards, resigned his office, in some indecision of mind apparently, sold his property, and at the age of forty entered the monastery himself.

The monastery was no retreat from the world for Gregory however. Hardly had he entered the community when the monks elected him their Prior. Soon the bishop, Pelagius II, sent him as his Legate to the Bishop of Constantinople, called the Patriarch. Considerable rivalry had existed between the bishops of old and new Rome, and Gregory's mission was to make their relations easier. He was not able to reconcile the differences permanently, though he won the personal esteem of all whom he met, and he learned how to proceed later when relations between the two bishops became his responsibility. In 585 he was recalled to Rome, and became virtually Secretary of State. To this period belongs the best known story about Gregory. While walking in the market place he saw a group of fair-haired boys, obviously captives waiting to be bought as slaves, for slavery still existed though the Empire was called Christian. He asked what race they belonged to, being struck by their fair complexion, and was told "Angli," "Angles," from once Christian Britain, now overrun by the heathen Angles and Saxons. "Non Angli, sed Angeli," he replied, "Not Angles but Angels," and he resolved then to go to convert the Angles into "co-heirs with the angels." But he himself was prevented. One story says that he had actually started with the aged bishop's permission but was recalled at the indignant insistence of the people who already regarded him as their next bishop. In 590, at any rate, he became Bishop of

Rome, the first monk to reach that dignity, only sixty years
after the founding of the Benedictine Order.

Gregory did not forget his resolve to convert the
heathen Angles and Saxons after he became bishop. He
chose a man named Augustine, who had succeeded him as
prior of the monastery in Rome, and sent him with a band
of monks to England. They started on their mission not
without great fears and misgivings. When they reached
Gaul the monks sent Augustine back to Rome begging to
be allowed to return. The English monk, Bede, a century
later, wrote, "They were seized with craven fear and
began to think of returning home rather than go on to
a barbarous, fierce and unbelieving nation whose very
language they knew not." Bede also gave Gregory's reply,
"Gregory, servant of the servants of God, to the servants
of the Lord. It were better not to begin good works than
to think of turning back from them when begun. It is your
duty, beloved sons, to accomplish the good work with
God's help which you have started on. . . . God Almighty protect you with His grace and grant me to see
in the eternal country the fruit of your labors."[1]

Augustine and his monks landed in Kent in 597 and
met the heathen king, Ethelbert, who was married to a
Christian Frankish princess, Bertha, and had allowed her
to bring her chaplain to England with her. Ethelbert refused to meet the monks inside a building for fear of witch-
craft; so he sat under a tree and waited for their approach.
They came bearing a great crucifix and singing a litany
"for their own salvation and theirs on account of, and to

---

[1]Bede's *Ecclesiastical History of the English Nation*, Book I, chap.
XXIII.

whom, they had come," as Bede said (Book I, chap. XXV). Ethelbert gave them the ruined church of St. Martin in Canterbury for their use and, the following Whitsunday, he and most of his court and followers were baptized. On Gregory's orders Augustine returned to Arles in Gaul to be consecrated Bishop of the English. In consequence Augustine is usually reckoned as the first Archbishop of Canterbury. Thus, Bede wrote (Book II, chap. I), Gregory "by his own zeal converted our, that is, the nation of the Angles, from the power of Satan to the faith of Christ, and him we may and rightly should call our apostle."

If Gregory did not forget the Angles in the market place neither did he forget that they were slaves. In freeing two of his own slaves, he wrote a decree which should have ended forever the institution itself: "Since the Redeemer and Creator of the world willed to incarnate Himself in humanity, to break by the gift of freedom the chains of our bondage, it is to act well and fairly to restore their original freedom to men whom nature made free, but whom the law of nations has bowed under the yoke of slavery. Wherefore we make you, Montanus and Thomas, servants of the Holy Roman Church, which we also serve by the help of God, from this day free men and Roman citizens." That Gregory was alive to the social responsibility of his office, we may gather from the story that, even though Italy was devastated by famine as a result of the Lombard raids, when a single beggar died from hunger he refused to say Mass as though he were responsible for the man's death.

Gregory was forced to act as civil ruler of Rome and

much of Italy. He made treaties with the Lombards, and to insure that they lived up to their agreements paid them money out of the income of the bishop. With a touch of irony he called himself Paymaster to the Lombards. When the Eastern Emperor rebuked him for usurping the functions of the Imperial official, who had himself made no move to govern Italy, Gregory replied that the peaceful settlement he had won from the Lombards was respected even by them, and on that basis it must be accepted.

Gregory was not only a political administrator, he exerted authority in the Church also. He claimed to be the chief bishop in the Church, and as such to govern his brother bishops in Italy. One was forced to do penance before Gregory, saying, "I have sinned against God and the most holy Pope Gregory." The Patriarch of Constantinople at this time began to call himself Ecumenical (*i.e.,* Universal) Patriarch, and Gregory vigorously protested. He sought to rebuke the Patriarch by taking for himself a title of great humility, *Servus Servorum Dei,* "Servant of the Servants of God," a title still used by the Bishops of Rome. This title, however, did not lead Gregory to give up his claim to be the successor of St. Peter and therefore by Christ's appointment chief bishop and Father, or Pope, of the whole Church.

We have over eight hundred letters from Gregory's voluminous correspondence. He wrote to people throughout Europe on all manner of subjects. He composed a famous work, the *Pastoral Rule,* containing detailed advice and counsel as to the life and pastoral work of his clergy. There are those who say no better book of the sort has ever been written. Gregory insisted that all Church

accounts be kept with great care, and he set the example
with the papal revenues. His name is used most frequently
today in connection with church music for he is considered the father of the Gregorian Chant. Probably he
simply took what was already done, and had it codified
and arranged in some order. But by so doing he fixed for
all time the "proper," that is, official, music for the Mass,
and the Psalms of the Daily Offices.

While Gregory was concerning himself about the conversion of the heathen Angles and Saxons there was
another similar attempt being made by missionaries from
the Church in Ireland. Ireland had been Christianized in
the fifth century by St. Patrick, a Briton, the son of Christian parents of pre-Anglo-Saxon stock. In his *Confessions*
he tells us his father was a deacon and his grandfather a
presbyter. He lived in Wales or in the neighborhood of
the Severn River. When he was sixteen he was captured
by pirates and sold into slavery in Ireland. He later escaped and seems to have studied in Gaul whence he set
out to convert his late captors. Because of his connection
with Gaul some have supposed him to be a native of that
country, but he is now known to have been a Briton.

The Church in Ireland became the center of a flourishing civilization long before Gregory's mission went to
England. It was cut off from Europe, however, by the
Anglo-Saxon conquest and developed a life and customs
of its own. The original tribal organization of the country
became the basis for a monastic system in which bishops
were subordinate to the communities themselves. The
remains and manuscripts of the Irish Church of the sixth
century show Ireland to have had the most advanced

civilization in Europe at the time. Several Irish monks even became missionaries to parts of Europe already considered Christian. One Columbanus (543–615) left Ireland several years before Gregory saw the slaves in the market place, and, with a disciple named Gall, revived the decadent Christian communities in Brittany, as he later did in Burgundy. He finally died in Italy in a monastery he founded at Bobbio on a strict Irish model. He is said by historians to have rekindled Christian devotion and civilization in Gaul and Italy. The great monastery of St. Gall on Lake Constance owed its origin to him.

It was another Irish monk with a similar name, Columba (521–597), who set out to convert the English. He founded a monastery on the island of Iona on the west coast of Scotland about the year 565. He was intent first on Christianizing the heathen Picts and Scots, but, at the moment St. Augustine of Canterbury was landing in Kent, Irish monks from Iona were moving southward into England. The two missions worked independently of each other for years, though not without friction. Co-operation was not made easier by Augustine's contention that he should settle all matters himself as Pope Gregory's representative. The Irish had hardly heard of Pope Gregory. There were pagans enough to be converted to keep both missions busy for awhile, but often their spheres of work overlapped. When Edwin, the heathen king of Northumbria, married a Christian princess from Kent, he allowed a Christian priest, Paulinus, to enter his realm. Edwin was baptized, but soon killed, and whatever Christian work had been established was destroyed by the heathen. When the heathen usurper was himself killed,

Edwin's son, Oswy, sent to Iona for Irish monks to re-establish Christianity. Aidan came and was given Lindis-farne, or Holy Isle, off the northeast coast of England for his monastery. At Whitby, also on the northeast coast, a famous dual monastery, one for men and one for women, was presided over by a woman, the Abbess Hild. Finally in 664 a Synod at Whitby officially joined the two missions, Irish and Roman, from which the Church of England grew. A new archbishop, Theodore of Tarsus, a Greek, succeeded in bringing the two missions into close union by his conciliatory approach and his organizing ability.

One thing is noteworthy about the Christianizing of England; both the Irish and the Roman missions were monastic, and monasteries continued the centers of learning and missionary zeal that they were in Ireland and in Italy. Wearmouth, founded in 674 by Benedict Biscop, soon possessed a great library. The monk Bede, father of English history, lived in the monastery of Jarrow, in Northumbria. From the monastic schools of York the monk Alcuin, before the year 800, was brought from England by Charlemagne to found a Christian educational system in his Frankish Empire. In 690 St. Willibrord went to Frisia (Holland) where he worked for fifty years, becoming first Archbishop of Utrecht and the Apostle to the Netherlands. St. Boniface, or Winfrith, went to Rome in 720 and was made a bishop with orders to go to Thuringia and Bavaria. He is the Apostle to Germany, and was martyred in Frisia in 754. Thus Gregory's mission to England, augmented by Celtic or Irish zeal, won most of northern Europe to Christianity. The Danish invasions of England in the ninth century drove the Church there underground in a new age of persecution, and so cut off further missionary work, but until then the English Church was the center of Christian missionary zeal.

As Gregory the Great lay dying, a rival religion was being born in the Arabian peninsula, a religion of the sword, which within a hundred years practically wiped out the Christian Church in Asia Minor, Egypt, and North Africa, swept through Christian Spain, and threatened to conquer all Christian Europe. The swift rise of Mohammedanism sent terror into the hearts of men throughout the West. By the year 732, just a century after the death of its founder, Mohammed, this new missionary faith sought an entry into France. The Mohammedan, or Moslem, advance was stopped in a seven days battle that raged over the country between the cities of Tours and Poictiers in October of that year. The man who stopped it was Charles Martel (the Hammer), who was the chief minister, or Mayor of the Palace, to the decadent Frankish the way for an alliance between his successors and the kings. His victory saved Christian Europe and opened bishops of Rome which in turn began a new era in Europe.

From now on until the sixteenth century we may speak of Christendom, meaning the Europe which sought to find a working and workable unity of the political and the spiritual. The Church had made its place as the spiritual power in Europe. When the old Empire in the West crumbled it oftentimes had been forced to assume political power also. Now the political force was becoming strong again, though except in theory there never was one State, as the Roman Empire had been. The two powers, the Church and the State, must work out a way of sharing dominion, and the history of the Middle Ages is the history of this attempt. In every conflict, as in every agreement, between the spiritual ruler, the pope, and the temporal rulers, whether king or emperor, the ultimate ideal was such a unity as would leave each its proper sphere. But naturally enough in practice each often seemed to feel that European peace and unity would best be served by his being the controlling partner.

The alliance between the Frankish kings and the popes was aimed directly at the Lombard kingdom in Italy. This alliance was suggested to Charles Martel's son, Pepin the Short, by St. Boniface, who was not only a missionary, but also something of a statesman. Boniface told Pepin, who was fretful at being the power behind the throne, that the pope felt that the man who was king in fact should be king in name, and he agreed to anoint Pepin king with the pope's blessing. In return Pepin would force the Lombards to leave the pope in peace. The anointing of Pepin greatly impressed the Franks; it was a more awe-inspiring ceremony than their old military custom of raising the new king on a shield, and it gave the Church new dignity and influence among them. Pepin routed the Lombards, and forced them to hand over some of their land to the pope, thus beginning the temporal power of the papacy. This power, lost in 1870 at the unification of Italy, was restored by Mussolini in 1929 as part of his Concordat with the Vatican, though the actual domain was much curtailed.

Pepin's son Charles, or Charlemagne, confirmed the alliance with the pope, and sought the papal aid for his own aims and ambitions. He dreamed of restoring the Empire in the West. He conquered the Saxons and other Teutonic tribes east of the Rhine and established his authority in some fashion over most of western Europe, excluding the British Isles. Charles' ideal, as has been said, was what he believed St. Augustine advocated in the *De Civitate Dei,* that is, a truly Christian Empire. The pope's ideal came from the same source, though he would have given a slightly different emphasis to his interpretation. However the two agreed on the ideal, and on Christmas Day, in the year 800, Charles was crowned Emperor by Pope Leo III in Rome. Leo had a great mosaic erected to commemorate the event in the Church of St. John Lateran, his cathedral, showing Charles and himself kneeling and receiving from St. Peter the symbols of their respective authorities. Charles called himself "the representative of God who has to protect and govern all the members of God," and he considered the pope one of these members. The pope could maintain, however, that since Charles had waited for the pope's assent before assuming the title, and actually had accepted the crown at the pope's hands, the Imperial power was derived from the spiritual. Herein lay material for future conflict between popes and emperors.

For two hundred and fifty years after Leo III, however, the popes were dominated by the secular rulers. The so-called Holy Roman Empire came into being in 962 when Otto the Great, of Germany, was crowned by the pope, and Otto tried to restore the papacy to dignity and honor, but without success. In 1046 a well-intentioned priest in Rome, John Gratian, whose one single concern was to redeem the office from further degeneration, bought the papal dignity and title. This buying of the highest office in the Western Church, even for a good purpose, was the measure of the depths to which the office had fallen. Henry III, German, or Holy Roman, Emperor, intervened to depose John Gratian, known as Gregory VI, and restore the papacy to worthy men, but unfortunately the Germans who filled the office could not survive the malaria of the Roman climate.

The Abbey of Clugny, a reformed Benedictine community with over three hundred dependent houses throughout Europe, became the ally of the Emperor in these attempts at reform. The influence of Clugny was particularly strong in the man who came on the scene as adviser to Gregory VI (John Gratian), and who later became pope himself. His name was Hildebrand, of lowly Lombard or German descent. Hildebrand supported the attempts on the part of Gratian's successor, Leo IX, to force the clergy to give up their wives or mistresses and to remain celibate. He was also the guiding influence when Nicholas II (1058–1061) first placed the papal election in the hands of the College of Cardinals, which consisted of the principal clergy, bishops, priests and deacons of the city of Rome, "saving the honor and respect due to the Emperor." This method of electing a pope has persisted to the present day. Alexander II (1061–1073), the direct choice of Hildebrand, blessed the invasion of England by William of Normandy, under Hildebrand's inspiration, hoping to be in a position to control more directly the Church in England. William had no intention of allowing any outside power to be superior to him, however, and, while he promised to pay "Peter's pence," he refused to acknowledge the pope as his overlord, and he laid down limits to be observed by the pope in Church matters. Hildebrand, after being the advisor of popes and the moulder of their policies for years, finally in 1073 was made pope himself. At the funeral of Alexander II, so it is said, some one in the crowd set up the cry "Hildebrand, Pope," and the cardinals were forced to agree. He took the name of Gregory VII.

Hildebrand is known best in history for his quarrel with Henry IV of Germany, and the dramatic scene before the castle at Canossa, where Henry stood as a penitent, barefoot in the snow, suing for the pope's pardon. Henry had made bishops of various of his supporters, with no thought of their fitness, and had himself inducted them into their office. The pope protested that he alone had the right to invest bishops with the symbols of their authority. Bishops had become secular as well as spiritual officials, and both popes and temporal rulers therefore claimed to be their proper superiors. Henry's Synod of German bishops pronounced Hildebrand deposed from the papacy, but Hildebrand replied by excommunicating Henry and releasing Henry's subjects from their allegiance, and many of Henry's own bishops forsook him. A meeting of the Diet of the Empire was called at Augsburg to elect a successor to Henry, and Hildebrand set out to attend. Henry met him at Canossa in the Alps, and by going through the motions of penitence forced the pope to lift the ban of excommunication. Both emperor and pope knew that the papal triumph was more apparent than real, and this may account for the three days that Hildebrand kept

Henry waiting. He was trying to find a way to avoid accepting the show of penitence, but he was unable to do so. Henry showed his true attitude when, several years later, he took the city of Rome and set up an anti-pope.

It would be a mistake to think of Gregory VII as one who sought power simply for its own sake. He was a reformer, though not a very loving one, full of zeal and determination; his friends called him *Sanctus Satanus*—Holy Satan. "I have labored with all my might," he wrote, "that the Holy Church, the Bride of God, our mistress and our mother, should recover her honor and remain chaste and free and catholic." He died in 1085 in exile, however, saying, "I have loved righteousness and hated iniquity, and thus I die." The particular issue in the quarrel between Hildebrand and Henry, usually called the Investiture Controversy, was settled by a compromise in the next century, in England in 1107, in Europe generally in 1122. The kings or emperors agreed to renounce the right to invest bishops with any but the symbols of their temporal authority; investiture with ring and staff being reserved to the pope or his representative in the king's presence. Bishops were not to be appointed by the temporal rulers, but to be elected freely by the clergy, though again the ruler was to be present. This latter ruling did not define the position of the pope in the election of bishops, nor did it cover the larger question of the respective authority of popes and kings.

A conflict over this authority raged in England between Henry II and Thomas à Becket in the twelfth century. Becket had been Henry's bosom friend and chancellor, and opponent of the Church, but now was Archbishop of Canterbury and defender of the Church and clergy against Henry. He sought to prevent the king from controlling the election of bishops, and from confiscating for his own treasury the revenues of bishoprics so long as they remained vacant. Henry wanted the clergy subject to the jurisdiction of the ordinary courts, and hoped to prevent any appeals to the pope. These were provisions of the Constitutions of Clarendon (1164), which Thomas and the other bishops had accepted, but later repudiated with the pope's blessing because they made the Church subordinate to the State. This repudiation angered Henry who exiled Becket and only permitted him to return when threatened with excommunication. Becket came home amid popular rejoicing, and appears to have been regarded as their defender by the poor and helpless. He had no intention of giving in to Henry, however, and his first act was to excommunicate some of Henry's supporters. This was the occasion for Henry's reputed outburst, "Is there no one to rid me of this pestilent priest?" Three men rushed to Canterbury and murdered the archbishop. Henry refused to accept responsibility, but he did public penance and withdrew the demands of the Constitutions. Thomas à Becket became the most revered saint of England during the rest of the Middle Ages, and his shrine the richest and most popular.

The papacy reached its height however in the next generation in the person of Innocent III who became pope in 1198 and died in 1216. He was of proud and noble Guelf blood, of the patriotic Italian party which opposed the Imperialist Ghibellines. He became a cardinal at twenty-eight and pope at thirty-seven. His first words as pope, "Who am I that I should sit in state above kings and occupy the throne of glory?" summarize his character and his conception of the office. He was a shrewd and able administrator, a careful scholar, and easily the master of kings and emperors. He forced Philip Augustus of France to put away his second wife in favor of his first whom he had divorced with the assent of the French bishops. Philip threatened to turn Mohammedan—"Happy Saladin, he has no pope above him"—but he thought better of it.

In 1208 Innocent compelled John of England to accept his nominee as Archbishop of Canterbury, but he had first to lay the realm under Interdict, which meant that no sacraments could be administered except in case of imminent death. John held out until 1212, when Innocent commissioned Philip Augustus to invade England. The king then agreed to pay the arrears of "Peter's pence," and to yield England to the pope as part of the papal domain, as Italy was, and to receive it back as the pope's vassal. When Stephen Langton, the man who became archbishop at Innocent's demands, led the barons of England in demanding that John sign Magna Charta (1215) he was severely censured by the pope because he and the barons had not first consulted Innocent. The first Article of Magna Charta says distinctly that the Church shall be free, *Ecclesia Anglicana libera sit*. To the archbishop, and perhaps to the nobles, this meant free from royal interference in the election of bishops. It is a nice speculation whether Innocent suspected the vagueness of that clause might be interpreted to mean "free from papal jurisdiction." Several times in the thirteenth century at any rate gestures were made in that direction, notably when in

1253 Grosseteste, Bishop of Lincoln, refused to make a nephew of the reigning pope a canon of his cathedral.

Innocent was not only a great pope in political affairs; he was the pope who befriended Francis of Assisi, as we shall see, and encouraged the evangelical piety of the Mendicant Friars, those of St. Dominic as well as those of St. Francis. Innocent also promoted reforms among the clergy, and was notable for the favor he showed the Jews. In November, 1215, he presided over the Fourth Lateran Council, said to have been the most representative Church Council since Nicæa, though the Greek Church was not represented. Innocent did not wholly achieve his ideal, which was the complete spiritual unity of Christendom, a truly Christian Commonwealth of Europe with the papacy as an international tribunal or world court. The function of the Church, and especially of the papacy, was to keep Europe on the right path. It was not Innocent's ideal that was amiss, but his method. In feudal times he thought and acted in feudal terms, and in practice he was able to make good his claims, as "Christ's Vicar" to control the kings of Europe. But he controlled them only because he was powerful enough to do so, and either he did not see the weakness of this line of action or he was not able to find a way out of the situation.

In the twelfth century the Crusades, or armed expeditions to rescue from the Turks the places made sacred by Christ's ministry in Palestine, united Europe under the cry *Deus vult*—"God wills it"; but they were not conspicuously successful, perhaps again because the method was wrong. The Seljuk Turks had become masters of Palestine in the eleventh century and had challenged the

Christian Emperor in Constantinople. In spite of the fact that the Church of the Eastern Empire with the Patriarch of Constantinople as head had severed relations with the Church of the West in 1054, and received reciprocal excommunication from Rome, the Emperor of Constantinople around the year 1070 appealed to the pope for aid. When Hildebrand became pope he answered the appeal with a call for a Holy War against the "Infidels" who dominated the "Holy Places."

Actually, the First Crusade was "preached" in 1095 by Peter the Hermit, acting for Pope Urban II. Godfrey de Bouillon, the leader, was apparently a sincere man bent on recovering Jerusalem and other shrines from the hands of unbelievers. In 1099 Jerusalem was captured after great slaughter, but Godfrey refused to be crowned king where his Saviour had worn a crown of thorns. After Godfrey's death in 1100, his successors were not so punctilious. The Second Crusade in 1146 failed because of poor planning and treachery, and the Third, occasioned by the loss of Jerusalem to Saladin the Saracen leader in 1187, ended in a working agreement between Saladin, a noble high-minded man, and Richard the Lion Hearted of England. This is the Crusade of Scott's novel, *The Talisman*. The Fourth Crusade, in the time of Innocent III, was sidetracked to Constantinople, where fighting between the Western Europeans and the Greeks of the Eastern Empire, Christians all, ended in the establishment of a Western or Latin Empire in Constantinople which lasted for fifty-seven years. Already the Crusades had failed of their purpose, and even lost their sense of purpose.

The Children's Crusade was the epitome of the whole

movement. Religious enthusiasm and unbounded devotion, that relied on God's miraculous intervention to achieve what seemed a good end, came to a disastrous conclusion in death and slavery worse than death for innocent and impressionable children at the hands of the Turks, with the connivance of so-called Christian shipowners and merchants. "The Jerusalem that now is, and is in bondage," in St. Paul's phrase, seemed more important than "the Jerusalem which is above, which is the mother of us all." The noblest and most saintly figure in the whole movement, Louis IX (1226–1270), called St. Louis, died on the shores of Africa while on a crusading expedition. Louis had gone on a Crusade in his early life, been captured and ransomed. After a long reign fruitful of much good, he felt that he must go again. His close friend and adviser, de Joinville, refused to accompany him saying that Christ was better served among His people at home. St. Francis of Assisi, a contemporary of St. Louis, was to show a better way, and Roger Bacon, the English Franciscan Friar of the thirteenth century, had as clear vision when he wrote, "Nor are unbelievers converted in this way, but killed and sent to hell. The rest, who survive the wars, and their children, are more and more embittered against the Christian faith . . . and are infinitely alienated . . . the faith did not enter this world by arms, but by simple preaching."

Chapter 9

ST. FRANCIS OF ASSISI

---

*"As poor, yet making many rich,
As having nothing and yet possessing all things"*

THE THIRTEENTH CENTURY, whose opening years saw
Innocent III bring new prestige to the papal chair, has
been called "the greatest of centuries," and not without
reason. It was the century in which Gothic architecture
began to reach out to new achievements. Churches, monasteries and cathedrals, reflecting the devotion alike of
builders and worshippers, reached greater heights, literally
and figuratively. The art of making stained glass and of
carving in wood and stone kept pace with the architectural
development. Before the century was over two Italian
painters, Cimabue and Giotto, turned to the life of St.
Francis for their inspiration and devoted their talents to
religious art. In literature the French poetry of chivalry
reached its final form, and Dante by his *Divina Commedia*
and other works helped form the Italian language from
medieval Latin, and thereby began Italian literature. The
educational systems of the Middle Ages reached their
culmination in the twelfth and the beginning of the thirteenth centuries with the rise of the universities. Monas-

tery schools had already been replaced in importance by cathedral schools, and from these in turn the universities sprang. Paris had been famous for theology since the time of Abelard in the twelfth century, and when the thirteenth century opened Bologna had become the center for law and Salerno for medicine. Oxford and Cambridge, the latter founded in the thirteenth century, helped England to keep pace with the intellectual development of Europe.

This very splendor of the thirteenth century throws into sharper contrast the failure of the Church to minister to the lives and needs of ordinary men. Innocent III had a dream, so it was told, in which the Church's walls were falling and he was unable to hold them up until he was joined by an insignificant-looking man in a brown habit. Thus men tried to account for Innocent's friendship for St. Francis and his Little Poor Men. But it was no dream; it was sober fact. The Church had been so occupied with its position in the world, its authority, its patronage, and its wealth, that it had become involved and compromised. Life had become comparatively secure again for monks as for society, and security made for complacency and lack of concern for the welfare of the common man. The poor became poorer, lacking food and homes often, and, surrounded by filth and disease, these sufferers were largely unshepherded. There was need for a new vision to send men out into the highways and city streets, to farm-hovels and slums, where God's children were neglected, and where sin and evil reigned. But the vision would demand of those who heeded it the acceptance of poverty for themselves and the willingness to live among the degraded, even as Christ who "for our sakes became poor." Such a vision came to St. Francis of Assisi, and he obeyed.

He was not born Francis, however, nor was he born poor. His father, Pietro Bernardone, one of the new and prosperous merchant class, was an importer and a dealer in cloth. He was a thoroughly practical man, out to make money, and his only dreams were of larger warehouses and finer fabric. Pietro's son was born while he was in France buying cloth, and on his return Pietro found that the boy's mother had had him christened with the biblical but dull name of Giovanni (John). Pietro allowed himself one venture into fancy by refusing to use the boy's given name, and calling him instead, "Francesco," "his little Frenchman." No one had borne the name before, and its use is among Pietro's claims on posterity. He took a secret pride in observing that his boy's companions called him Francesco too; and this was enough to make him open his otherwise tightly closed purse whenever Francesco wanted money. The open purse was the way to social position with the sons of the petty nobles and, if money would help, Francesco should not lack it.

Apparently Francesco was of one mind with his father in this particular. He was not much interested in the business, but Pietro did not require him to be. He was the popular and gay leader of the crowd of carefree young dandies out for a good time. No one supposed that they were dissolute or immoral, but they lost no opportunity to enjoy life as they found it, even though they disturbed the slumbers of the older and the more staid in Assisi. It was the fashion generally to copy French ways and manners, even Pietro did so. Troubadours and their courts of love were the models, and Francesco, "the little Frenchman," led the way.

The town of Assisi was passing through trying times when Francis, to return to the English spelling, was a young man. In the century before, the Emperor Barbarossa and his son Henry VI had seized many Italian towns, Assisi among them, and had handed them over to German nobles, who drew their revenues from the cities. In Assisi the German count lived in a castle outside the town and meddled not at all in the life of the citizens. Henry VI died in 1197, however, and Innocent III became pope in 1198. Innocent forced the German count to withdraw, and the citizens, afraid that the pope's representative would be a more demanding master, tore down the castle walls and with the stone built a wall around the city. They then began to make demands on the nobles who lived in the great houses at one end of the town, and who were landlords of the fields and farms as well as of property within the city. When the nobles refused their demands, the people threatened to tear down their houses also and add the stone to the city wall. The neighboring city of Perugia took up the cause of the nobles, but the citizens of Assisi remained firm in their demands and refused to repair or pay for whatever ruin they had already inflicted. Fighting broke out between the two parties and dragged on for two years. Then in 1202 the citizens of Assisi were decisively beaten in a battle at Ponte San Giovanni, and the son of Pietro Bernardone was among the prisoners taken to a Perugian dungeon.

Francis probably was not a very good soldier. He

could be brave enough, but he could also be foolhardy; and the war to him and his companions was but another lark. Even in prison he refused to be downcast. After all, they would be ransomed, he told his companions, and in the meanwhile why be discouraged? He composed new songs for them to sing and planned new escapades when they got home again. For himself, this war had given him a foretaste of what he was going to be, a great prince. His father gladly paid his ransom, and he returned to Assisi. Almost immediately he fell ill of a malarial fever, and when he recovered he was surprised to find his spirits lacking along with his strength and vitality.

Soon the opportunity presented itself for him to become a great prince. The pope was engaged in a war in southern Italy, and Walter de Brienne was enlisting an army. His father equipped Francis as if he were to lead the army, and no doubt gave occasion for many a jest about the merchant's son turned soldier, going to the wars to win honor and rank. But after he had started Francis decided that he would not go on with it. He awoke one night to hear a voice saying this military life was not for him. Giving away his horse and equipment to one who could use them, he abandoned his ambition, and, to his father's consternation, returned home. No one thought him a coward, but madness might account for this strange action, and his companions received him back with sidelong glances. He tried to enter into the old life but there was no zest in it, and he was not his old self. He was his father's bad investment. He gave a banquet in the way he always had, but he grew thoughtful in the midst of it. His comrades asked him if he were in love, to which he replied, "Yes, but with a lady unknown to you—My Lady Poverty." Then they knew he was mad.

What was he talking about, My Lady Poverty? Francis could not have explained. He had no inclination to enter a monastery or study for the priesthood. He only felt a vague disquiet about his way of living, his lack of serious purpose, and the fact that many people were in dire need of what he literally threw away in gay abandon. This almost subconscious feeling he could express in none but romantic terms, for that was the habit of his thinking. It was not just romance, as the rest of his life clearly shows, but he himself did not yet see where he was being led. He went to Rome on a pilgrimage, showing that he sensed the religious element in his uneasiness, and while there, on impulse, exchanged clothes with a beggar and sat at the door of a church so that he might experience for himself destitution and poverty. On his way home a leper met him face to face, and, in horror at the sight of the half-decayed features, he was about to hurl a coin and run when something stopped him. He stepped up to the leper, embraced him and begged his pardon.

If a moment must be found to mark his conversion, this meeting with the leper was that moment. Lepers were considered by Church and society to be the living judgment of God on sin. They had no civil rights, could not own property, nor even dwell among living men. When they were discovered to have the dread disease they were officially pronounced dead, and the burial service actually held. Henceforth they were outcasts, living on alms in wretched shelters outside the towns. Families were allowed no intercourse with them. They must carry a bell to ring constantly as a warning, and they were expected to leave the highroad when any one approached lest they contaminate the passers-by. Church and society agreed on this, and never worried at the bitterness and misery that filled the souls of lepers. Suddenly this bitterness became clear to Francis. Suddenly in this leper, as in every leper he later met, he saw Christ, who "was despised and rejected of men."

Next day he went to Mass at the small ruined Church of San Damiano, which appealed to him because it was in such decay, its altar and sanctuary so poorly appointed. He meditated long on the crucifix, and the Figure there seemed to say to him, "Restore my fallen house." He took that to mean rebuild the church itself, and on impulse again, with no thought apparently that his father would object, he sold some cloth from his father's storehouse and gave the proceeds to the priest who was in charge. The priest, for fear of Pietro, refused to use it and left the money on a window ledge inside the church. Pietro ranted and raved; so much so that Francis disappeared for a while. Then one morning a great commotion arose in the streets of Assisi, and Pietro went outside to see what was happening. There came his son, dressed in rags, unkempt and unwashed, followed by a crowd that hooted and jeered. Beside himself with rage, Pietro rushed out and dragged Francis into the cellar and locked him in. When his father was away from home his mother let him out, and Francis went back to San Damiano. Francis tried to pacify Pietro by offering him the money from the sale of the cloth, still unused in the niche where the priest had put it. His father pocketed the money but was not satisfied; he wanted his son to go back and stop this madness, or he wanted no son.

Pietro was prepared to disown Francis, and he went first to the civil court and then to the bishop. The bishop, after talking to both, advised Francis to renounce all claim to his inheritance. Clearly there was no point where the minds of Francis and his father could meet. In a dramatic gesture Francis stripped off his clothes, and laid them at the feet of his father, saying, "Till now I have called Pietro Bernardone my father. To him, who with so much trouble gave me this money and raiment, I now return them. Henceforth I have no desire but to serve God and say, 'Our Father who art in heaven.'" If there is an unfilial sound about the words it must be remembered that Francis did not say them without a pang. He was an affectionate person; but by now he recognized that his vague disquieting dreams were the voice of God, and God's service for him demanded perfect freedom. For some weeks he went into seclusion in the hills, living on charity or what berries he could find in the woods, enduring the chill of the nights and the heat of noonday with equal unconcern. Some robbers asked him who he was and he replied "The herald of a great King." They beat him and took away the clothes he was wearing. He went on, singing, until days later some one gave him an old cloak. He stopped at the leper houses when he found them, and ministered to the needs of the worst sufferers, finding in so doing what to him was "perfect joy."

Francis was still haunted by the command "Restore my fallen house," so he went back to Assisi to begin work on the little Church of San Damiano. This time he had no money nor way of securing it, but he begged stone from his old friends and with his own hands carried what he got to the place. Slowly he began to repair and rebuild the church. When that was done, he turned to repairing another little church, "Santa Maria della Angela," called *Portiuncula*—"the little Portion." The name appealed to him, and the church soon became the meeting place for all those who joined him. He persuaded a priest to say Mass there from time to time, and one day the words of the Gospel seemed meant especially for him, "Go preach, saying, 'The kingdom of heaven is at hand.' Heal the sick, cleanse the lepers, raise the dead, cast out devils; freely ye have received, freely give. Provide neither gold, nor silver, nor money, nor scrip for your journey, neither two coats, nor shoes, nor staff. For the workman is worthy of his meat" (Matthew 10:7–10). Most of this was his way of life already, he had only one thing more to do, "Go, preach." His preaching was little more than conversations in the market place or roadways, witnessing to men the joy that was his, but his sincerity and lack of self-concern moved them. And the enthusiasm and gaiety with which he became the *Poverello*, the "little poor man," was not less than that with which he had become the leader of the revels. For him it was a consuming adventure, now he was a troubadour of God.

Soon followers were drawn to him, the first, Bernard of Quintavalle, a man of some wealth, who had been a companion in the revels. One morning these two with Peter Cathanii, a Doctor of Laws, went to the Church of St. Nicholas in the public square, and there sought in the Gospel Book for some command. First they opened to the words of Christ spoken to the rich young man, "Go, sell

all thou hast and give to the poor . . . and come follow
Me"; next they read, "Take nothing for your journey,
neither staff nor scrip, nor bread nor money"; and lastly,
"If any man will come after me, let him deny himself."
Francis turned with glee to his companions saying, "Brothers, this is our life and rule, and that of all who shall join
our company. Go and fulfill that ye have heard." This was
the beginning of the Franciscan brotherhood; no house,
no lands, no resources, no rule save that in the Gospels,
spontaneous, happy, and withal earnest and sincere. Eight
days later came Giles, son of a small farmer, saying,
"Brother Francis, I want to be with you for the love of
God." Francis introduced him to the others with the words,
"See what a good brother the Lord has sent us." The story
of their meeting a poor beggar woman who asked for
alms is typical of the simplicity and charm of the early
days of the brotherhood. They had no alms, and Giles was
troubled; he wanted to give something but he did not want
to bother Francis, who was lost in thought. Suddenly
Francis turned and said, "Let us give the poor woman thy
cloak," at which Giles gladly parted with it, and in great
peace of mind they went into Assisi.

Francis was not thinking of an order however. He
merely thought that a few "little brothers" would join
him in his wandering, living the life of the poorest and
most unfortunate, and showing forth by the love in their
own lives that God is love; working where they could for
food and a place to sleep, accepting charity where they
must. Giles and Francis went off together, lay preachers,
without authority or dignity even. The name which
Francis loved, the "Lord's Players" (*Joculatores Domini*)

probably came from this period and was given in amusement by the peasants. Others were not so kindly in their judgment, but called them fools and fanatics. When the number became twelve the Bishop of Assisi called Francis to ask him what he meant to do. The bishop thought the life too severe, and he was also disturbed by the lack of dignity and the lack of authority. He had heard the name "the Lord's Players" and he thought it might be used blasphemously. He begged Francis to enter an order and take his brothers into a monastery.

Francis, moved by the bishop's urging, yet unable to follow his requests, decided to go to Rome and get the pope's blessing. In Rome he found opposition; his life of simplicity put that of the clergy and monks to shame. Only one among the cardinals defended him, but finally Innocent III allowed him to adopt for his company the title "Penitents of Assisi" or "Fratres Minores" (Little Brothers). The "Minori" were the common people in Italy. Francis was deliberately using the word. Monks and priests were largely drawn from the upper classes, the "Majori," the great. Unfortunately they had also become content to minister to the great. Francis was going out to minister to the least, the commonest of men, and he meant to identify himself and his brothers with those to whom he would minister. The Rule was simply what they had been practicing already and Francis was the living embodiment of it:

"The Rule and life of the brothers is this: namely, to live in obedience, in chastity and without property, and to follow the teaching and in the footsteps of our Lord Jesus Christ who says: 'If thou wilt be perfect, go sell what thou hast, etc.' "

"And all the brethren shall be clothed in poor garments and they can patch them with sacking and other rags with the blessing of God: for our Lord says in the Gospel 'they that are in costly apparel . . . are in kings' houses.' "

"The brethren who know how to work shall work and exercise the same craft which they know, if it be not against their soul's salvation and they can honestly exercise it. . . . And for their labor they may receive whatever is needful, except money. And should it be necessary, they may go asking alms like other brothers."

"Let all the brothers endeavor to follow in the humility of our Lord Jesus Christ and let them remember that of all the world it behooves them to have nothing. . . . And they ought to rejoice when they consort with rude and despised persons, with the poor and weak and sick and lepers and those who beg by the wayside."

"When brothers go through the world they shall carry nothing by the way, neither purse nor scrip nor bread nor money nor staff. . . ."[1]

Thus in the year 1210 the Franciscan Order came into being, but it was still no order in any formal sense to Francis. It was merely a brotherhood of those who were willing to sacrifice everything to follow Christ. New brothers offered themselves; among others, Juniper the simple cobbler, and Leo a young priest, of all most beloved by Francis. In Assisi the brothers lived in an abandoned leper asylum, or built huts around the chapel of the Portiuncula. But Francis did not intend his brothers to have settled abodes. They had been necessary for monks when everything else was unsettled, but they had become a source of weakness, an insulation against the world.

[1]This is taken from the version of the first Rule as given in Father Cuthbert's *St. Francis of Assisi*, pp. 103–106.

Franciscans must be able to move about and move about fast. They were to seek out those who needed them, even pursue them if necessary, and they must have no encumbrances or impedimenta. "The world around him was . . . a network of feudal and family forms of dependence. The whole idea of Francis was that the Little Brothers should be like little fishes who could go freely in and out of the net. They could do so precisely because they were small fishes, and in that sense slippery fishes. There was nothing that the world could hold them by; for the world catches most of us by the fringes of our garments . . . a man had to be thin to pass always through the bars and out of the cage; he had to travel light in order to ride so fast and so far."[2]

The life Francis dreamed of for his brothers, however, was too hard for many who were drawn to him by his charm and sincerity. Twice a year, at Whitsuntide in late spring, and at Michaelmas in September, they were to come together to consult with him. In 1218 or 1219 more than five thousand came to the Chapter of the Mats, so called because they slept on mats of willow branches for beds. Some of them felt that they should have a more settled abode and a longer Rule, and they appealed to Cardinal Ugolino who was present. Francis' reply was firm:

"My brothers, my brothers, the Lord called me by the way of simplicity and humility, and showed me in truth this way of life for me and for those who will believe and imitate me. And therefore I will not have you name unto me any Rule, whether of St. Benedict, or St. Bernard, nor

[2]G. K. Chesterton, *St. Francis of Assisi*, pp. 117–118.

any way and form of life except that which the Lord in his mercy hath shown and given unto me. The Lord told me that He wanted me to be poor and foolish in this world, and that He willed not to lead me in any other way."[3]

Soon after the Chapter of the Mats Francis, having settled things in his own mind and being oblivious to the grumbling of the brothers, went to Egypt to see if he could not show the Crusaders there a better method of accomplishing this end. The Sultan actually allowed him to speak to him of Christ, and then sent him back to the Crusaders' forces as harmless. Suddenly he had a disquieting message from Italy. Still there were demands for changes in the Rule, and the authorities in the Church thought there was need for more organization. In Francis' absence some of those closest to him had been forced to go into hiding. He returned for the Michaelmas Chapter of 1220 and at once resigned his position, feeling that no longer were the brothers held together by ties that bound them to him. He sought out Cardinal Ugolino, his first friend in Rome, and agreed to write a new Rule. Peter Cathanii was his choice to be the new head, but Peter died, and at the Whitsuntide Chapter of 1221 Brother Elias was made "Minister General." Elias was a student of the Law and a man of ability, but he split the brotherhood in two. So long as Francis lived there was no open conflict, but after the founder's death, the break became apparent.

The Rule of 1221 simply reaffirmed the old emphases, and added certain explanations. It was no new Rule, and hence did not satisfy the discontented. In 1223 the Rule

[6]From the "Mirror of Perfection," quoted in Father Cuthbert's *St. Francis of Assisi*, p. 270.

came up again, and Francis was persuaded to rewrite it.
He did so only to have Elias lose it. Patiently he returned
to the task. Francis said that the brothers must follow his
Rule or he would have them leave the Order. The new
and final Rule changed little of the admonitions to poverty, but it bore the marks of defeat. From this time until
his death Francis counted for little in the life of the Order.
Nor did he wish to do so. The pope approved the last
Rule, in which poverty and simplicity were enjoined, and
Francis could still live by it and prove it practical, whatever others might do.

The Christmas following this Chapter of the new Rule
he spent in retreat near the mountain village of Greccio.
There he had one of his friends build a shelter with a
manger in it and an altar. To this shelter came all the
countryside, and any brothers who would, for the Midnight
Mass of Christmas. Francis was the deacon at the Mass.
He had been persuaded to be ordered deacon, but he
would never allow that he was worthy of the priesthood.
After he had read the Gospel, he preached, speaking so
movingly and vividly of the stable at Bethlehem that
men said the image of the Baby in the crib came to life at
his touch.

In 1224 after the Whitsuntide Chapter had commissioned Brother Agnello of Pisa to establish the Order
in England, Francis retired again to the mountain retreat
of Monte Alverna. More and more he desired solitude,
where he engaged in the deepest and most intimate prayer
and communion with his Saviour Christ. Now on Monte
Alverna, or La Verna, he was to undergo his most poign-
ant experience. He had planned to keep a forty days fast

before the coming of Michaelmas (September 29). On Holy Cross Day (September 14) he saw before him the figure of Christ in the form of a seraph, but he also saw as he gazed that the figure was crucified. As he grieved over this, from the figure there seemed to come a piercing of his hands and feet and side, and as the vision disappeared he became aware of the wound-prints in his own body. These marks are called the *Stigmata*. What the experience was we cannot fully know; in part the welling up of his own deep sorrow over his brotherhood, in part his being able to comprehend what it meant for Christ to bear the Cross for His brethren. With it all came a great peace and a great sense of victory. He had not failed after all, as Christ had not failed. Brother Leo was near by, and to him and Rufino the mystery was revealed. With gladness and the old joy, Francis riding a donkey because of weakness, they returned to the Portiuncula.

From then on he was able to go about very little, though he started out again. Afflicted with a serious disease of the eyes, which was only aggravated when the doctors prescribed that the nerves be cauterized, he had to permit himself to be carried back to Assisi, carried back by a roundabout way lest the Perugians should try to capture him and hold his body for ransom. Now, weary and ill, worn out from too great demands on his "brother body," he was brought to the bishop's palace. At the end of the summer, however, he asked to be taken to the Portiuncula, and there dictated his will, ending with the words:

"And the brethren shall not say: this is another Rule; for this is but a remembrance, admonition and exhortation and my testament, which I, Brother Francis, your little one, make for you my blessed brethren, to the end that we may observe in a more Catholic way the Rule which we have promised to the Lord . . . as the Lord has given me to speak and write the Rule and these words simply and purely, so shall you understand them simply and purely, and with holy doing observe them unto the end."

He asked to have his tunic removed, and to be laid naked on the ground that he might die in the direst poverty. His brothers began to sing, at his command, his *Canticle to the Sun* to which he added at this time the last strophe. Then he blessed the brothers and had them break bread, and each eat a scrap, and with the words, "Welcome, Sister Death," he "entered eternity singing." This was October 4, 1226. In less than two years the Church had officially declared what every one had already known, that Francis was a Saint; and Elias had begun the building of a great church to enshrine his poor body.

To attempt to sum up the qualities that make Francis the figure of such power and charm is well-nigh hopeless. His complete unconcern about things that to most men seem important strikes one immediately. He was literal about "taking no thought for the morrow," but this is really the same trait that made him the young scrapegrace of Assisi, and the pride of his father's heart. His contempt for possessions followed this carefree nature, "If we had possessions we should also need arms to protect them." Better not have a book, even a prayer book, than be puffed up with the pride of ownership. His emphasis on poverty was his way of saying that people are more important than property or possessions.

To Francis all life was good because God had made it.

He had Christ's feeling for the world around him. He called the sun "brother" and the moon "sister" with complete sincerity. His sermon to the birds expresses the simplicity of his love for nature. He once said he wanted to see the Emperor to ask him to "publish an edict against catching my sisters, the larks." Francis valued above all things the element of joy in Christianity. He said once to a novice, "Before me, and before thy brothers here, always show a face shining with joy. It is not fitting when one is in God's service to have a somber face or a chilling look."

Francis discouraged learning because he feared that his followers would become mere scholars, arguing over fine points which matter not at all. Some of his followers used this as an excuse for intellectual indolence. An amusing story is told of a Franciscan friar who was being lodged for the night at a Benedictine monastery. When grace was said, *Benedictus benedicat,* he thought it referred to St. Benedict and was a slur on Francis, so he screamed out, *Franciscus franciscat;* which was bad manners and worse Latin. Many Franciscans have left their names among intellectual leaders, however, none more illustrious than Roger Bacon in Oxford.

Francis was greatest, and his gift to men most notable, at the center of his life, his religious experience. Machiavelli, the Italian writer of the fourteenth century, said that Francis "saved Christianity and wrecked the Church," meaning probably that for Francis following Christ was simpler and more informal than churchmen had conceived it to be. Yet Francis himself was a loyal and obedient son of the Church, and his Testament bears witness to his faith in the Church and in priests. The *Stigmata* was to him the culmination of the life he had led "in Christ," to use St. Paul's phrase. It is not the only phrase of St. Paul's that comes to mind. "I bear in my body the marks (*stigmata* in Greek) of the Lord Jesus" (Galatians 6:17). Francis had always striven to bear the marks of his Lord, and beyond doubt he entered into His experience in a way that is beyond us. Some have objected that, whereas Christ said "Follow me," Francis changed it to "Imitate me." Francis' mind was not subtle enough to sense a distinction, or perhaps it was too subtle. He was not given to rationalizing. He saw in the literal statements in the Gospel the challenge that he must accept. For him it was the way to "follow," and for as many others as would.

Francis felt that men in his day needed to be recalled to simplicity, as indeed they did. He saw no need for great riches for any one, though he did not condemn others for having them. If some men were to live on charity, he understood that others must have something to give in charity. He founded a Third Order for men and women living in the world, enjoining them to live simply and with concern for others. He himself, however, wanted to be absolutely at the disposal of his Lord; and he saw no other way than absolute poverty. Yet his poverty had a social purpose, as the name, "Friars Minor," indicates; it was for the sake of God's poor.

THANKSGIVING OF ST. FRANCIS FOR ALL CREATED THINGS, USUALLY CALLED THE CANTICLE OF THE SUN

O Most High, Almighty, good Lord God, to Thee belong praise, glory, honour and all blessing!

Praised be my Lord God with all His creatures, and especially our brother the sun, who brings us the day, and who brings us the light; fair is he, and shining with a very great splendor: O Lord, he signifies to us Thee!

Praised be my Lord for our sister the moon, and for the stars, the which He has set clear and lovely in heaven.

Praised be my Lord for our brother the wind, and for air and cloud, calms and all weather, by the which Thou upholdest in life all creatures.

Praised be my Lord for our sister water, who is very serviceable unto us, and humble, and precious, and clean.

Praised be my Lord for our brother fire, through whom Thou givest us light in the darkness; and he is bright, and pleasant, and very mighty and strong.

Praised be my Lord for our mother the earth, the which doth sustain us and keep us, and bringeth forth divers fruits, and flowers of many colors, and grass.

Praised be my Lord for all those who pardon one another for His love's sake, and who endure weakness and tribulation; blessed are they who peaceably shall endure, for Thou, O Most Highest, shalt give them a crown!

Praised be my Lord for our sister, the death of the body, from whom no man escapeth. Woe to him who dieth in mortal sin! Blessed are they who are found walking by Thy most holy will, for the second death shall have no power to do them harm.

Praise ye the Lord, and give thanks unto Him, and serve Him with great humility.

(Matthew Arnold's translation.)

BANQUET OF THE LADY POVERTY WITH THE BROTHERS

"And having made all things ready, they constrained her to eat with them, but she said: 'First show me your oratory, your chapter house, your kitchen, your dormitory and stable, your fair seats, your polished tables, and your great buildings. For none of these things do I see, only I see you merry and joyful, overflowing with gladness, filled with consolation, as though you looked for all things to abound according to your desire.' And they answered and said, 'Lady, our Queen, we, thy servants, are weary with the length of the way, and thou coming unto us hast had no slight toil. Let us eat together first if it is thy will, and so strengthened, all things shall be fulfilled according to thy behest.'

" 'Be it as ye speak,' she says. 'But now bring water, that we may wash our hands, and towels wherewith we may wipe them.'

"They made haste and offered her the half of a certain earthen dish full of water, because there was not a whole one. And pouring water upon her hands, they looked this way and that for a towel. And when they had not found one, one of them offered the tunic which he was wearing, that with it she might dry her hands. . . . Then they led her to the place where a table was prepared, and when she was brought thereto, she looked and saw nothing but three or four crusts of barley and bran bread laid upon the grass. . . . And the Lady Poverty gave orders to bring cooked food on dishes. And behold, one dish was brought full of cold water, that they might all dip their bread in it. For there was no abundance of dishes there, nor many cooks. She asked that at least some fragrant uncooked herbs of sweet savour should be supplied to her, but as they had no gardener, and knew nothing of a garden, they gathered wild herbs in the wood and set them before her. And she said: 'Bring a little salt, that I may salt the herbs, since they are bitter.'

" 'Wait a little, Lady,' say they, 'until we go into the town and bring it to thee, if, haply, some one will give it us.'

"And she said: 'And have you a little wine here?'

"They answered and said: 'Lady ours, we have no wine. . . .'

"After they were filled, rejoicing more in the glory of their poverty than they would have in the abundance of all things . . . they led her to the place where she should repose, because she was weary. So upon the bare ground she flung herself down in her scant raiment. She asked also a cushion for her head, and they forthwith brought a stone, and set it under her; but she slept with most quiet and sober slumber, and rose up in a little while and asked to be shown the monastery. And they led her to a certain hill and showed her the whole world, as far as she could see, saying: 'This is our monastery, Lady.' "

(Giovanni Parenti, Sacrum Commercium,
chapter XXII.)

Chapter 10

THE HOLY CHURCH

"Hora novissima, tempora pessima"

IT MIGHT SEEM enough for one age to have produced
St. Francis, but he does not exhaust the religious contributions of the thirteenth, "greatest of centuries." St. Dominic,
contemporary of Francis, was as great though not so immediately appealing perhaps. Of Spanish birth and descent,
he too was a loyal son of the Church. He saw with sorrow
how many of the children of Mother Church were stray-
ing away into paths of "heresy," and he sought to find
some way to lead them back into the Body of Christ.
Heretical groups were numerous in the Middle Ages, and
the Church was ever on guard to prevent them from gaining ground. One reason there had been so much pressure
put on St. Francis to organize his brotherhood was the
fear that it might otherwise stray away into heresy. Some
Franciscans did this very thing within the century. Dominic
felt that the chief reason for heresy was the failure of
priests to teach their people adequately, and therefore
he founded a teaching brotherhood, called officially the
Order of Preachers, or more generally the Dominican
Order. Dominic was so impressed with the Franciscan vow

of poverty that he made his preachers into another Mendicant, or begging, Order. The Dominicans wore a white habit, and over it a long black cloak, hence in England they came to be called Black Friars to distinguish them from the Franciscans or Grey Friars who wore a habit of undyed wool. Almost immediately the Dominicans entered the teaching field in Paris and Bologna, and they were prepared to move into all the universities of Europe as they came into being. Their chief contribution in the thirteenth century, however, was made through St. Thomas Aquinas, who belonged to the second generation of Dominicans.

Thomas was born in the town of Aquina near Naples in the year 1225. He was destined to be a monk when he was still a small boy, not because his parents were particularly religious but because they wanted to control the great Benedictine Abbey of Monte Cassino, where the Benedictine Rule had first come into existence. If Thomas entered this community, when he was old enough they would see to it that he was elected abbot. As a boy in the monastery school he disturbed the monks by asking such questions as "Who is God?", "Where is He?" The Abbey of Monte Cassino was destroyed by the Emperor Frederick II, however, and Thomas forced to return home. His family then sent him to the University of Naples where he came in touch with the newly founded Dominican Order. He was attracted to them at once and at eighteen decided to join, but his family would not hear of it. To be abbot of a great Benedictine house with its revenues and influence was one thing, and a desirable thing; to be a begging friar in a new Order with neither property, status nor dwelling place was quite another, and a slightly disgraceful, thing. Thomas started secretly with several companions to join the Order in Paris, but his mother discovered the way he meant to take and sent his older brothers to kidnap him and bring him home. They locked him up and fed him on bread and water, but he persisted in his intention. They sent a beautiful woman to his room to tempt him to forget his vow of chastity, but Thomas seized a burning brand from the fire and rushed at her with a bellow of rage. She fled, and Thomas burned a great cross on the wall to mark his victory. Escaping from his family at last, he went to Paris and later to Cologne to attend the lectures of the most illustrious Dominican of the day, Albert the Great.

Thomas was a huge man physically, and a silent one on most occasions, absorbed in the problems he was trying to solve and intent on them only. His fellow students in Cologne called him "the dumb ox of Sicily"; they thought he did not understand anything of what was being said, at least he gave no sign of doing so. One day a kind-hearted companion tried to help him by beginning an explanation of a certain point only to find himself hopelessly involved and unable to continue. Thomas took up the discussion where it had been left and finished it in an abler manner than any one thought possible. The master overheard and set Thomas a particularly difficult question to discuss before the class next day. Thomas covered all sides of the problem so completely that the master said to the others, "I tell you the dumb ox will bellow so loud that his bellowing will fill all Europe." Thomas soon returned to Paris to lecture himself, and so well and clearly did he do so that he came to be called the Angelic Doctor, meaning that his intellectual ability was more than human. His absorption in his thoughts and problems increased; once he had been bidden to dine with Louis IX of France, "St. Louis," and as the dinner proceeded, Thomas fell into his usual silence and no one noticed him. Suddenly with a great blow on the table that made the dishes rattle and ring, Thomas said in a loud voice, "That will finish the Manichees." He had been pondering an argument and had forgotten where he was. The king, instead of being angry, sent some one to Thomas to take down the argument at once lest he forget some of the steps.

At the University of Paris Thomas found that the problem that occupied all minds was one of accommodating new learning to old faith, a perennial problem really though expressed differently in each age. Aristotle's logic, which had come to Europe in the twelfth century and furnished Abelard with new teaching material, seemed to many to destroy the Christian faith and creeds. The task of harmonizing the Church Fathers and Holy Scripture on one hand with Aristotle's emphasis on reason and logic on the other had not been served particularly well by Abelard, who sought largely to use Aristotle to set off his own brilliance. Aquinas tried to fulfill a more constructive end. He was a thorough believer in the power of human reason, a Rationalist in the correct sense of the term, and at the same time a devout believer in the creeds, a man of faith. Faith and reason were to him complementary, not contradictory, and every article of the faith was to be submitted to the test of reason. Thomas was sure that while the truths of Christianity could not be discovered by reason alone, none could be found that defied reason.

The two great works in which he set out to prove his contention are called the *Summa Theologica,* and the *Summa contra Gentiles.* In them he treated exhaustively all the articles of the Christian faith and in the process formulated definitions that have determined all Christian thinking subsequent to him. Some of the definitions have been strongly disputed, but they are none the less important. Whatever one believes about the authority of the Church or of the Bible, or thinks about the sacraments, purgatory and the communion of saints, sin and justification, one must go back, as all the sixteenth century reformers, both Catholic and Protestant, did, to the definitions of St. Thomas Aquinas. His works are still the textbooks of Catholic theology in the Western Church, and today his influence is growing through the rebirth of Thomism —or the teaching of St. Thomas; so well did he answer with the aid of human reason his own boyhood question, "Who is God?"

Thomas made one other noteworthy contribution to the Christian faith and life. In 1264 a new feast was established in the Church, the Feast of Corpus Christi. The Institution of the Lord's Supper, or the Holy Communion, or the Mass, remembered as it is and was in the midst of Holy Week on Maundy Thursday, must quickly be put out of men's thoughts because Good Friday immediately follows. Therefore it seemed well to set apart another day when the great Memorial could be properly kept, and the day picked was the Thursday after Trinity Sunday when the special days in the Church year had been concluded. Special Scripture and Psalms had to be selected for the offices and for the Mass, and special hymns composed. This mission was entrusted to Thomas and he wrote the hymns, "O Saving Victim" (*O Salutaris Hostia*), "Thee we adore, O hidden Saviour" (*Adoro Te devote*), and "Now my tongue the mystery telling" (*Pange lingua*) with its closing stanzas beginning, "Therefore we before Him bending, this great Sacrament revere" (*Tantum ergo*). The theologian and logician could write devotional poetry of great beauty, and say in verse what another Thomas, called à Kempis, in the next century said in prose in the *Imitation of Christ*, or what St. Thomas the Apostle had said at the first Easter, "My Lord and my God."

The greatness of St. Thomas Aquinas lay in the constructive nature of all he did; it is indeed this quality of constructiveness that makes the thirteenth century great. The following two centuries, at least until the second half of the fifteenth, may not be so described. In the intellectual field the method of disputation itself, in the hands of lesser men, degenerated until Scholasticism, as the method is called, came to connote a barren method of argument that often becomes no more than mere quibble. At the beginning of the fourteenth century two Franciscans, Duns Scotus and William of Occam, disputed the conclusions of Aquinas and ended in the position that even though some articles of the creed were contrary to reason, or might be considered so, they, nevertheless, were to be held on the authority of the Church as matters of faith. Scotus has given to the English language the word "dunce," which was used by his opponents, unfairly perhaps so far as his ability was concerned, to describe his arguments. He may be said to mark the beginning of the deterioration of medieval Scholasticism, argument for the sake of sharpening one's wits and not to discover truth. Not until the Renaissance of the late fifteenth century was there a resurrection of reason, and then the revival of learning, as it is often called, was largely divorced from religion and the Church, except, as we shall see, in the case of England and Germany.

The fourteenth and fifteenth centuries were centuries of degeneration in the papacy itself, beginning in 1309 when the French kings forced the popes to live in Avignon in France. Boniface VIII, who was pope in 1300, tried to establish over temporal rulers the same supremacy that Innocent III had succeeded in doing, but he found himself no match for Philip the Fair of France or for Edward I of England. The pope died in 1309, largely as a result of the ill treatment he received at the hands of Philip's soldiers, and the "captivity" of the papacy which followed lasted for seventy years. The seventy years ended in a worse state of affairs. In 1378 the reigning pope returned to Rome on temporary business matters and suddenly died there. The Roman people demanded that the cardinals who had accompanied him elect a new pope immediately, and that he should reside in Rome. The King of France forced the cardinals in Avignon to elect a successor to the dead pope who should continue to live in France. Europe was divided into two camps behind the rival popes. After thirty years of the two successions a Church Council met in Pisa (1409) and deposed both claimants to the papal dignity, and elected a new and legitimate pope; but neither of the deposed would acknowledge the authority of the Council to act. Henceforth there were three popes until the Council of Constance (1415) settled this scandal but was unable to reform the papal court of corruption. As the fifteenth century progressed, the popes, already entangled in political matters, and lacking any particular sense of the moral responsibilities of their office, became so concerned with the literary and artistic awakening that they had little time for their religious functions. Some of them were literary men of ability, but often frankly immoral and irreligious, and the purpose of the papacy was forgotten by them.

In England one result of the "captivity" and the schism was a strong anti-papal movement, which, by acts of Parliament, gave the king control over the elections of bishops, forbade appeals outside the realm, that is, to the pope, and limited the amount of taxation that could be levied by the Church. The clerical mouthpiece of this movement was John Wycliffe, a priest of the Church in England, who has been called "the morning star of the Reformation." Some of his ideas and emphases seem to us to have foreshadowed those of the reformers of the sixteenth century, but Wycliffe was a thorough Scholastic by training and method of thought and we read modern meaning into his words at the risk of complete misunderstanding. As Master of Balliol College, Oxford, he accompanied John of Gaunt, second son of Edward III, to Bruges in an effort to find a working agreement with papal delegates as to the king's power over espiscopal elections, and the forbidden appeals to the pope. Wycliffe returned convinced that the Church should own no property and have no taxing power or any need for money at all, and he went on to say that the State should control all Church lands and property, even to the right to confiscate them. The pope and the Bishop of London, shortly afterwards appointed Archbishop of Canterbury, naturally condemned such views. The Peasants' Revolt of 1381 was blamed on him (as a later one in Germany was blamed on Luther) with the result that he lost the support of the nobles who, for reasons of their own, approved his views on Church property. Wycliffe saw rightly in the Church's wealth a cause for the loss of moral and spiritual power; but the remedy of State control and even confiscation was one too easily to be used by politicians and land owners to enrich themselves.

Wycliffe began to question the authority of the pope, first of all on the practical ground that there could not be two popes at once. When he was asked which pope he was willing to acknowledge, his answer was "the one who shows true holiness of life." He never made it clear however who was to determine this fact. By the test of holiness there might be no pope perhaps; but there would be no bishop nor priest either by that test, and no Christian for that matter. Wycliffe may have recognized that his test could not be applied, and therefore he made no move to secede from the Church. He does not seem to have visualized a Church without an earthly head, and he was a good Catholic who did not see how any individual could separate from the Body of Christ. It would be difficult to maintain that he was an individualist in religion; he was a sincere reformer who thought things out not too clearly perhaps, and who spoke in language that was violent at times.

He attacked the doctrine of transubstantiation in which the Church held that the bread and wine at the Mass were changed into the Body and Blood of Christ; but the object of his attack seems to have been the explanation as to how the change took place rather than the fact of the change. Himself a devout believer in Christ's presence in the Sacrament, he took quite literally the words, "This is My Body." Again he was practical minded; he feared that the ordinary man would be unable to distinguish between the "matter" of bread and wine and the "substance" or "form" of the Body and the Blood, and might fall into idolatry by adoring the "matter." He found fault with the Scholastic definition, as churchmen in England did in the sixteenth century, but he gave no lead as to how the truth he accepted might be expressed in clearer language. He continued to say Mass as he always had done, and died from a stroke while saying it in his parish church of Lutterworth. He was hardly a Protestant before Protestants in this.

In one matter Wycliffe made a contribution of lasting worth, he translated the Latin Bible, the *Vulgate*, into a rugged English that is reflected in many turns of expression in later translations. In all his thinking and speaking he had appealed consistently to the Bible as the source of authority, rather than to the Bible plus tradition plus the Fathers, which was the medieval practice. In this he anticipates the sixteenth century Reformers. His translation, in the hand and on the tongue of Englishmen, profoundly influenced English religious life in the fifteenth and sixteenth centuries. A Bohemian affected by Wycliffe spoke words that would have been accepted by the Reformers: "When I saw that many men carried with them everywhere the relics . . . of divers saints . . . I chose for myself the Bible as my relic, the companion of my pilgrimage."

One well-known Bohemian follower of Wycliffe was John Hus, a priest and professor in the University of Prague, and an ardently patriotic Czech. He was twice elected rector of the University, a fact which led the German students to withdraw in 1409 and found the University of Leipsic. Hus followed closely the teaching of Wycliffe, though in the matter of transubstantiation he remained silent. After the matter of the rival popes had been settled, the Council of Constance turned to reports of heresy, especially of heresy in Prague and in England. The body of Wycliffe was ordered dug up and burned and his ashes scattered. Hus was summoned to the Council and given the assurance of the Emperor that he would be allowed to return home even if he were found guilty. It did not occur to Hus that he could be condemned, but he was vilely treated, scarcely allowed to speak, imprisoned and finally presented with a series of statements, alleged to have been drawn from his writings, which he was to confess and then recant in their entirety. He refused to do this because he said he had not made some of them. In spite of the Emperor's word he was degraded from his priesthood, and burned as a heretic along with his books. Such an appeal to force to settle heresy, of which Hus was not the first nor yet the last victim, was also accepted by Calvin and other Reformers in the next century, and the Christian faith and life gained nothing thereby.

The rebirth of Greek culture in Italy in the fifteenth

century, called the Renaissance, was marked by a new emphasis on beauty and an appeal to the senses that struck those who came in contact with it as a complete reversal of Christian values and emphases. Moreover the effect this reversal had on some was to make them skeptical of any of the Church's teachings, and willing to discard the Church's moral standards. In Italy, especially in the papal court, such was the reaction. The medieval Church seems often to have held up an ascetic ideal that denied the dignity of human life, and pointed men to an other-worldly solution for their problems. The men of the Renaissance nowhere showed themselves more the products of the late Middle Ages than when they accepted this apparent other-worldly emphasis without question. It remained for the artists among them to remember the central statement about Christ in the Creed of Nicæa, "And was made man." At least Michelangelo, Raphael, and even da Vinci saw that the Christian faith involved no denial of human values, as the thoroughly human figures in their paintings of the "Madonna and Child" or of the "Crucifixion" show. Perhaps it was on the moral side that popes and the papal court, as well as nobles and men of letters, found Greek emphases preferable to Christian. At any rate the new learning became their consuming passion, and they failed to unite this to their religion, or to remember that their religion made moral demands.

It would be a mistake to assume from what has been said about the fourteenth and fifteenth centuries however, that all true religion was dead. If that were so no reformation in the sixteenth century would have been possible, a corpse cannot be reformed. Medieval Latin hymns produced in the monasteries are one index to religious vitality, as for example the *Jesus dulcis memoria* ("Jesus the very thought of Thee"), of St. Bernard of Clairvaux in the twelfth century, and the *Hora novissima, tempora pessima,* by Bernard of Clugny shortly afterwards, of which "Jerusalem the golden," and "The days are very evil" are well-known parts. These were the property of monks, but the people had hymns and other forms of devotion. In northern Europe particularly there was in common use a "Lay Folks' Mass Book" containing hymns and prayers and directions for participation in the Mass. Popular hymns were used through the service, such as the one for use at the elevation of the Host:

> "Praisèd be Thou, King
> And blessèd be Thou, King
> Of all Thy giftes good.
> And thankèd be Thou, King
> Jesus, all my joying,
> That for me spilt Thy Blood,
> And died upon the Rood.
> Give me grace to sing
> The song of Thy praising."

The Mystery and the Miracle Plays, and the later Morality Plays, of which *Everyman* is the most familiar example, served both as means of education and as expressions of devotion. The first use of them had been distinctly educational when dialogues were introduced into the Mass at Christmas and Easter, dialogues between the shepherds of Bethlehem or the angels and the women at the Tomb. The Rosary was introduced by St. Dominic in the thirteenth century as a form of devotion for the ignorant and the sick who were unable to concentrate on the services.

In Holland the Brethren of the Common Life owed their origin to the piety and zeal for Christian education of Gerard Groote, who died the same year as Wycliffe (1384). The *Imitation of Christ* by Thomas à Kempis, which was referred to in connection with the hymns of St. Thomas Aquinas, was produced in one of the schools of this brotherhood in the fifteenth century. À Kempis was a monk, but he was a good monk. His piety was medieval, but it was good medieval piety. Akin to the Brethren were the German mystical associations, usually called the Friends of God, which grew and spread among the common man. Mysticism admits of no precise definition, but it is chiefly marked by the insistence that men can come close to God in prayer and meditation if they will cultivate that side of their life. The associations were formed to help the members do this. The *Theologia Germania*, which profoundly influenced Martin Luther, was produced by this movement though its author is unknown.

Two fourteenth century English poets give evidence of a vital religious life in spite of degeneration in the Church and in the monasteries. Geoffrey Chaucer in the *Canterbury Tales* had among his pilgrims to the shrine of Thomas à Becket a monk and a friar who were untroubled by their vows, but he also drew the picture of a faithful parish priest who,

> "Christes lore, and His Apostles twelve
> He taught, but first he followed it himself."

William Langland's *Vision of Piers Plowman*, though less artistic, is perhaps nearer the life of the ordinary man.

Piers is an English peasant with a little learning and religious training who bemoans the lot of poor men and the failure of monks, but who sees Christ walking English fields "in a poor man's apparel," and who believes rich and poor are blood brothers because Christ shed His blood on the Cross for all men. This was good simple medieval piety, and it comes very near being good gospel piety also. Religion was by no means dead in the fourteenth and fifteenth centuries, but we have to look beneath the official, and what often is miscalled the historical, life of the times to discover the vitality that existed. It was this contrast that produced the Reformers of the sixteenth century.

Chapter 11

MARTIN LUTHER
AND OTHER REFORMERS

"My conscience is bound by the Word of God"

THE RENAISSANCE in northern Europe, especially in England and Germany, was more interested in the study of the Greek New Testament than in the pagan Greek classics. Therefore the northern revival of learning was distinctly religious and Christian. By far the most illustrious leader north of the Alps was Desiderius Erasmus, who hoped for a reformation of the Church but sympathized not at all with the methods of the Reformers of the sixteenth century. He followed, unconsciously perhaps, Wycliffe's insistence that the Bible, the New Testament in particular, should be the guide and rule. He valued the Church, its life and sacraments, and he was a man of real personal piety, if we may judge by his book on the Christian life, called *Enchiridion*. On the other hand he knew from personal experience in a monastic house the weakness and degeneration of the Church and monastic clergy, and he hoped to reform these by turning the light of publicity and reason on them.

Erasmus was born out of wedlock in Rotterdam, in

the year 1466, as near as can be estimated. His father appears to have entered the priesthood just before the boy's birth. As a child Erasmus went to a school of the Brethren of the Common Life in Deventer, where he learned the value of simple piety and acquired his love for learning and study—the two ideals the founder of the brotherhood, Gerard Groote, as we saw, desired to instill. Before Erasmus was grown, his uncle forced him, much against his will, to enter an Augustinian Priory, and he came to despise monks and all their ways. He was allowed to go to the University of Paris to pursue further studies, and there he mastered the Greek language. In 1498 or 1499, he went to England at the urging of a young English scholar in Paris and began teaching Greek at Oxford. The Archbishop of Canterbury gave him a yearly income which he drew for the rest of his life, and he made the friendship of all the English scholars of his day, including Prince Henry, later to become Henry VIII. Erasmus himself was much influenced by the Christian humanism of John Colet, dean of St. Paul's Cathedral and founder of St. Paul's School in London. Perhaps Colet is the link between Wycliffe and Erasmus in their emphasis on the Bible, for he had already stirred Oxford by his lectures on St. Paul's Epistles. Erasmus in turn influenced Sir Thomas More, later to become Lord Chancellor of England, and the author of *Utopia*, a satirical description of an ideal commonwealth that still leaves us wondering what the author really meant. More was to die for his loyalty to the pope, and to become one of the most saintly figures in England in the sixteenth century. Erasmus wrote his famous satire on the monks, by which he hoped to set Europe laughing at them, the *Praise of Folly*, in More's house in London, and the Latin title, *Moriae Encomium*, is a punning compliment to his host.

Erasmus left England and made his way to Basle in Switzerland, where he joined the Froben brothers in their printing house. He saw the great value of the newly invented printing press in spreading knowledge, and he hoped thereby to reform abuses in the Church. He returned to England in 1509, the year the *Praise of Folly* was published, and spent two years or more in Cambridge holding the new Professorship of Divinity founded by the Lady Margaret, the mother of Henry VII. Back in Switzerland once more, he published his Greek text of the New Testament (1516), which was to influence Luther so strongly, and later his Latin *Paraphrases of the Greek New Testament*. Erasmus' way of reformation has been called the "way of amendment," and it had much to be said for it. But events moved too fast, or evils cried out with too loud a voice. He agreed with much that Luther said but deprecated his way of saying it, and in consequence he was suspected by both sides when the controversy broke out with violence. When he died in 1536, he may himself have understood with sorrow that the day for "amendment" was past, the day of revolution had come.

At the beginning of the sixteenth century, however, one would hardly have expected a violent revolution to upset the religious institutions of Germany. No land or people seemed as devoted to the Church and the pope. The country was filled with monasteries, the ordinary man and woman flocked to the churches for love of Christ and the Mass. Family religious life was of a high order: children learned the creed, the Lord's Prayer, and the Hail Mary in German at their mother's knee. Translations of the Bible into German were fairly numerous, though not of a high literary order, and were popular. German princes tended to encourage an anti-clerical attitude so as to add to their control over the Church, but they themselves were usually devout enough in the practice of their religion. It is not surprising therefore that, when Martin Luther posted his *Ninety-five Theses* on the door of the church in Wittenberg on All Saints' Eve, 1517, he was not raising a standard of revolt. He considered himself as faithful a son of Mother Church as any in the land. He had been brought up to love her ways, he had been nurtured in her teachings and sacraments, and he did not think his gesture in any sense disloyal. It was merely a challenge to his learned colleagues to debate a question that at the time had not been officially settled. The theses, in Latin, were addressed to the faculties of the universities and were in no sense a popular proclamation.

Martin Luther was born in 1483 in the village of Eisleben in Saxony, and christened Martin on November 11, St. Martin's Day, the day after his birth. Hans Luther, his father, was of peasant stock, but he had become the owner of a small smelting furnace and advanced a little in the world. In the village of Mansfeld, whence he moved shortly after Martin was born, he won a place for himself, and in 1491 became a Village Councillor. The life of young Luther was not an easy one; poverty was well known in the household, food was poor and sometimes scarce, the surroundings were hard and unrelenting. At school, as at home, the rod was not spared and the child was not spoiled. He learned his creed and Lord's Prayer and some simple hymns, and he learned also to fear witches and the devil and most of all Hell and the Judgment. He was taught to reverence the emperor and the pope as the constituted authorities in State and Church. When he was fourteen he went to Magdeburg to the school of the Brethren of the Common Lot, one of the mystical associations, and later to St. George's School in Eisenach. In the latter place he was a "poor scholar," which meant that he had to sing in the church choir for his food and lodging and was allowed the privilege of singing on the streets, in whatever spare time he had, to obtain extra pennies. In Eisenach he lived with a Frau Cotta who introducd him to life in a refined middle class household. The boy Luther showed marked ability in school, and his father planned big things for him in a worldly way and willingly made sacrifices for his son's advancement.

At seventeen Luther entered the University of Erfurt, and took his Bachelor's degree in a year, and his Master's three years later, 1505. At Erfurt, the foremost university in Germany, Luther became an accomplished lute player and something of a poet. He attained fluency and skill in the use of Latin, the language of his studies, as well as an acquaintance with Latin classical authors. He began the study of law to fall in with his father's dreams, but suddenly he gave up the law and entered a monastery of the Augustinian Canons. This step surprised his friends and angered his father, who saw all his dreams shattered at one blow. Luther said that it was fear that drove him into the monastery—and there was a large element of superstitious fear in his make-up—yet in the monastery his fear and desperation finally led him into the religious experience that transformed his life. The Augustinians held all the theological and philosophical chairs in the German universities of the day. Luther's superiors meant to make of him a theologian and a teacher, and he began to prepare for the priesthood. He was ordained in 1507, and Hans Luther came to his son's first Mass, entirely reconciled and bringing a gift to the monastery.

The monastic life did not bring to Luther peace of mind, however. His doubts and fears kept returning, and he spent much time in self-examination. The other monks thought they had a saint in the making in their midst, but the authorities wisely forbade his daily use of the confessional. He was growing more and more despondent when the Vicar General of the Order, Johann von Staupitz, came to Erfurt. Luther told him the fears that haunted him, namely that he was entirely outside the pale of God's love and nothing he did seemed to bring him closer. Von Staupitz apparently had known tender consciences before, and he set Luther to reading St. Paul's Epistles. He tried to show him that in a sense no man is worthy of God's love, and yet on the other hand it is possible to come into fellowship with Him if we trust His promises through Jesus Christ. What a man cannot do merely by multiplying his good deeds, he can do by wholehearted loyalty to God in Christ. This was the origin of Luther's teaching about the place of faith in a Christian's life. St. Paul had said. "The just shall live by faith," and Luther accepted that as the key to all Christian experience as it had been the key to his own.

Von Staupitz held a professorship in the new University of Wittenberg, founded by the Elector Frederick of Saxony, and in 1508 he brought Luther there to lecture on Aristotle. In 1511, in Rome on business for the Order, Luther was greatly interested in the ruins of classical civilization and in the relics and shrines of the Christian martyrs, but he was shocked by the worldliness of the papal court, and disquieted by the extravagances of pilgrims at the shrines. This latter experience revealed the mercenary nature of so much popular religion and had a lasting effect on his mind. In 1512 he succeeded von Staupitz as Professor of Theology in Wittenberg, having taken the degree in Theology at Erfurt meanwhile, and at once he included in his courses lectures on the Scriptures. He was a frequent preacher in the Castle Church, which served as a chapel for the University. He was soon made Sub-Prior of the monastery and District Visitor of the Augustinians in Thuringia.

In his lectures on the Scriptures, Luther used the Greek New Testament of Erasmus as soon as it appeared, but even before that his treatment differed from other lecturers on the Bible because the foundation of his teaching was a vital religious experience. We have to go back to this experience if we are to understand Luther's revolt against the current religious emphasis as revealed in the sale of Indulgences in Germany. He did not come into direct contact with the Indulgences because the Elector Frederick had forbidden their sale in Saxony. The thing that troubled Luther, however, was the theory that seemed to be behind them. The popular errors that a man could sin and buy forgiveness, which the Church certainly did not teach, were encouraged undoubtedly by the sellers of the Indulgences. The great teaching of St. Augustine, that God's grace, or free and loving mercy, was sufficient for every man and was all that could save the sinner, was being lost sight of, if not denied. Luther's opposition took the practical form of a challenge to debate, and it met instant response because of the practical results his opposition threatened to have.

Indulgences were, after all, very practical matters. Albert of Brandenburg, not old enough to become a bishop and yet already holding two bishoprics, had been permitted by the pope to become Archbishop of Mainz. To raise money to pay for this dispensation, he was allowed to sell Indulgences freely in Germany. Half of the proceeds of this sale was to go directly to the pope for the building of St. Peter's in Rome, the other half was to go to Albert who would give it to the pope as taxes. The chief salesman was a Dominican friar, named Tetzel, who seems to have been a master of the art of popular appeal. When the pope first heard of Luther's theses, he supposed it was simply a case of jealousy between the Dominicans and the Augustinians, and he requested the Vicar General of the latter to keep his monks quiet. Leo X was a member of the house of the Medici, and not particularly interested in or familiar with the religious issue. On becoming pope he is reported to have said, "Now that God has given us the papacy, let us enjoy it." What disturbed him most was the falling off of papal revenues.

At the annual Chapter of the Augustinian Friars in April, 1518, the theses were debated in a calm and friendly manner, and opposition to Luther's position made itself

felt, opposition that was stronger than Luther imagined.
He wrote a careful answer to his opponents, the "Resolu-
tions," addressed to the pope with a preface addressed
to von Staupitz, but he also began to write pamphlets in
German explaining his stand. The pope summoned Luther
to Rome in the summer of 1518, but the emperor and
the elector combined to have this cancelled, and the matter
was left to the pope's legate in Germany, Cardinal Caje-
tan. The legate was not so much interested in the truth
of the matter, as in forcing Luther to withdraw his statements without argument. But Luther could not withdraw
now even had he wished, for Germany was rallying behind him, and the question once raised must be settled,
not dismissed.

In June came the famous Leipzig debate with John
Eck, as he is usually known. Eck forced Luther to say
that John Hus, burned by a General Council at Constance
in 1415, was not wholly wrong. This meant that Luther
was in revolt against the Church since he had declared
his agreement with a pronounced heretic. The result in
Germany was to rally the young Humanists, as well as
the burghers and all German patriots, around him. The
result in Rome was to start in motion the machinery that
produced sentence of excommunication. While Luther
waited, he wrote the three famous Reformation Treatises.
The first, "The Liberty of a Christian Man," set forth his
belief in the priesthood of all Christians by reason of the
grace of God, given freely to all. The second, "To the
Christian Nobility of the German Nation," pleaded with
the German Princes to reform the Church, since clearly
the pope would not. The third, "On the Babylonian Cap-

tivity of the Church," set forth the errors and abuses that had crept into the official teaching in the centuries and asked for a return to the Gospel.

The Papal Bull, entitled *Exurge Domine*, from the words of Psalm 74, with which it began, "Arise, O Lord, plead thine own cause; remember how the foolish man reproacheth thee daily," was promulgated in the summer of 1520, and intrusted to John Eck to publish. The universities refused Eck admission, bishops raised technical difficulties, and many, Luther among them, declared they believed the Bull a forgery. John Eck was abused and satirized, and Luther finally invited the Wittenberg students to a public burning of the Bull in December, 1520. The crowd sang a solemn *Te Deum*, and then ran wild with enthusiasm. The Reformation had become Revolution.

Luther's protector, without whom he could not have held his own, was the Elector Frederick of Saxony, called the Wise. Frederick was a pious and determined man, thoroughly German in his attitude toward Italians, hence he refused to give Luther up to the Papal Court. Further, he was jealous of the rights of his new university, and meant to keep the persons of his professors inviolate. The pope was unwilling to offend Frederick at this time because Frederick was one of the seven electors of the Holy Roman Empire, the emperor was a dying man, and the pope was anxious to control the choice of a successor. When the Imperial elections actually came, the pope failed, though he tried, to prevent Charles of Spain, a devout Catholic and also the most powerful ruler in Europe, from becoming the Emperor Charles V. The one thing Charles hoped to do was to restore religious peace and unity. A young man of twenty-one, he met his first Diet of the Princes of Germany in the city of Worms in 1521. To this Diet he summoned Luther, under safe conduct, and there tried to bring the erring monk back into the Church's ways and teachings.

Luther's friends besought him not to go, reminding him of the fate of Hus, who also had an emperor's safe conduct. Luther was unmoved, and in spite of the risks was determined to present his case before the Empire. The scene in that old German city, whose people were always arrayed against their bishop and who now were strong for the young rebel, is described by eye-witnesses in exciting terms. After the emperor's charge had been read, Luther was permitted to speak, and the tenor of his remarks is summed up in his closing words, "My Germany will not allow me to recant." Then he added, "It is impossible for me to recant unless I am proved to be wrong by the testimony of Scripture or by evident reasoning. . . . My conscience is bound by the Word of God, and it is neither safe nor honest to act against one's conscience. God help me. Amen."

After some time had elapsed and several conferences with Luther had been held, one of which was a private audience in the nature of a confession by Luther to the Archbishop of Trier [Treves], Luther was ordered to go home. For twenty-one days he was to be safe, after that he was liable to be seized and put to death. Suddenly, however, he disappeared. Wild rumors of abduction by the papal delegate, murder in a deserted mine, and such, were circulated. The great nobles and ecclesiastics feared a league of peasants, burghers, and petty nobles. A ban in which Luther's writings were condemned was passed after Luther's friends had left Worms, but it only served to make them more popular. Men were assured that Luther was safe when new pamphlets by him began to appear. The Elector of Saxony, it became known, had ordered him spirited away to safety, and not even the elector himself knew where he had been taken. Luther was in the castle of the Wartburg, where he spent the next ten months translating the New Testament from Greek into German, thereby laying the foundation for the modern German tongue. The Old Testament he translated from the Hebrew later. Some of the followers of Luther in Wittenberg were moving too fast and too far, however, and as suddenly as he disappeared Luther reappeared in Wittenberg to curb the extremists, and to put an end to their methods of forcing reform. Perhaps the clue to the great influence of Luther was his unwillingness to move too fast. He was really a conservative, and he led people because he was never very far ahead of them.

Luther's conservatism on the other hand lost him the following of some who were sincere but radical reformers, and it led to the tragedy of his stand in the Peasants' Revolt of 1525. Germany had known such revolts before, and there were crying injustices and cruel oppression that needed reform. This time the peasants took Luther's words about liberty, and applied them to their condition. In the south they formed the Evangelical Brotherhood, which wrung concessions from their lords in an orderly manner. But soon bloodshed entered, and the revolt began to take on serious proportions. With its extreme form

Luther had no sympathy, but his name was being coupled with it in such a way as to alienate some of his followers among the princes. He was, moreover, horrified at the massacres. Finally, peasant though he himself was, he publicly repudiated the uprising and wrote a pamphlet, "Against the murdering thieving horde of Peasants," exhorting the princes to crush them. Perhaps it was inevitable, certainly it was a tragedy. Many of the common people joined the religious sects that were in revolt equally against Rome and Luther, and divided even further the forces of Christianity; and Luther became more and more suspicious of the judgment of the crowd and moved away from his early democratic ideals.

Luther found himself unable to join forces with a Swiss, Ulrich Zwingli, who had revolted against Rome and founded a free Church in Zurich. Zwingli, influenced by the Italian Renaissance, had entered a monastery, primarily, it seems, to cultivate his music. He became a priest and a chaplain of Swiss mercenary soldiers, some of whom served the pope. Zwingli felt that they were ill-used, and he first became concerned with such reforms. Later he widened his field to religious matters, and decided that nothing was to be accepted or retained in the Church unless it could be found in the Bible and especially enjoined there. Zwingli and Luther met at Marburg in a series of Colloquies but found themselves unable to agree over the words of Christ, "This Is My Body," "This Is My Blood." Zwingli took what became the extreme Protestant position that the words mean simply, "This bread stands for and is to remind you of My Body." Luther's position was very near to Wycliffe's, that is, he rejected transubstantiation but accepted the teaching that the Body and Blood of Christ were actually present. From Zwingli have sprung the Reformed Churches, Dutch Reformed, Reformed Church in America and others. He was killed in a battle between the Catholic and Protestant cantons of Switzerland in 1531. His followers were persecuted later by both Roman Catholic and Lutheran princes.

Luther had come to feel before this that the clerical rule of celibacy, which had been enforced often with such great difficulty, had no scriptural authority. Even then he might not have put his idea into practice personally except that a certain Katherine von Bora, one of a company of nuns who left their convent, appealed to him for protection. Luther is said to have assured her he would find her a husband only to have her intimate that he himself would be satisfactory. He married her in 1523 and their home life, with six children, was especially happy. Always poor themselves, they managed none the less to take poor students into the family. The dinner conversations of this group are the basis for the famous *Table Talk*, a document of great value in the history of the times as well as of Luther himself.

The actual Church that Luther founded, or that sprang from his views, showed all his conservatism and caution. With the help of his friend Philip Melancthon, who had translated his German name Schwarzerd, or "Black-earth," into Greek, he published a German Mass in 1526 which gave directions in German, and provided for communion in both kinds, that is, the laity were to receive both the bread and the wine. This had been one of the demands made by John Hus and was among the counts against him at Constance. German hymns, many of them old ones, but some new compositions, were introduced into the services. The Bible and the preaching of the Bible were to be the center of Lutheran practice. Luther had no objection to bishops, but he saw no great necessity for them, with the result that they disappeared in Germany in the Catholic sense, though the Lutheran Church of Sweden retained them. About such details Luther did not legislate, nor did he have authority to do so except his personal authority. He believed that princes should legislate for and arrange all matters in the Church, and this became a fixed principle in Lutheranism. It is the basis on which the final religious settlement, "The Peace of Augsburg," was made in 1555. Luther's early democratic ideals, as we saw, suffered a sad decline after the Peasants' Revolt, and of necessity this decline affected his views of Church government and orders. He never seems to have troubled much over organization or matters of ritual, however, leaving that to those who were concerned, or to the moment.

Luther's character and personality are easily abused and misunderstood. He was a monk who disrupted the Church; yet he did not set out to disrupt it, he merely wanted to reform it. It might easily be maintained that the pope and the curia disrupted it because they refused to consider any reforms, however obvious. He was a monk who broke his vows and married, but celibacy was simply a matter of discipline, as he knew, and not an article of faith. For him the vow ceased to be binding when it ceased to serve a social and religious purpose. His language often sounds coarse and crude to us, but ordinary conversation in the sixteenth century was crude, and moreover every chance word Luther spoke was copied down and preserved. Few men would be great by that test. He had a real mastery over language, however, and he helped form modern German by his translation of the Bible and his hymns, of which the best examples are *Ein' feste Burg ist unser Gott* ["A mighty fortress is our God"] and the Christmas carol, "Away in a Manger" which he wrote for his children. He made great mistakes, as in the Peasants' Revolt, but he was forced into conservatism by the fear of having everything destroyed. He was courageous when faced with danger. His reply to those who would keep him from Worms in 1521 is well known, "though there be as many devils at Worms as there are tiles on the house tops." He was the man of action which the times needed, and none other would have been effective.

Social and political matters, not least among them being the threat of the Turks to overrun Europe by way of the Danube, made a dead letter of the decree of the Diet of Worms (1521) by which Luther was outlawed and his teachings condemned. In 1526 a new Diet met at Speier which attempted to enforce the decree but the action was prevented by the Lutheran delegates. Another Diet met in Speier in 1529, however, which acted to enforce the decree of banishment, and the Lutherans drew up a "Protest" to this action. This is the origin of the word "Protestant," and hence strictly it refers only to Lutherans. Charles V had been absent from Germany during these years, but he returned in 1530 and called a meeting of the Diet at Augsburg where the statement of the Lutheran faith, that had been drawn up by Melancthon, was first made public. This statement has always been called the

"Augsburg Confession" because it was first issued in that place. The Diet of 1530 gave the Lutherans or Protestants until April of the next year to recant or be suppressed. The Catholic cause was still strong, and remained so, in southern and western Germany. The Lutheran princes of the north formed the so-called Schmalkaldic League to oppose forcible action. Thus Germany kept an armed truce which, several times after Luther's death in 1546, was broken by violent action. In 1555 the famous formula known as the Peace of Augsburg was evolved—*Cujus regio, ejus religio*—which may be freely translated, "the people must follow the religion of their prince." This formula made no provision for any except Catholics and Lutherans. Anabaptists, the forerunners of the modern Baptist Churches with their insistence on adult baptism by immersion, were constantly persecuted though after the suppression of the Peasants' Revolt in 1525 many disaffected peasants joined the sect. Zwinglianism could not be practiced in Germany either, nor could the new reformed doctrines that were coming out of Geneva in Switzerland, the doctrines of Calvinism.

John Calvin, founder of Calvinism, belonged to the second generation of Reformers. He was a Frenchman, born in Picardy in 1509, who took a degree in Paris at the age of nineteen. His father, who was legal adviser to the higher clergy of Noyon, secured the incomes of several clerical offices, employed curates to do the work, and used the remainder for his son's education. Such a procedure though irregular was common enough. Young Calvin left the College de Montaigu in Paris at the age of nineteen, at the same time that a Spanish ex-soldier, Ignatius de

Loyola, of whom we shall hear more, entered at the age of thirty-six. Calvin's father quarrelled with the Church authorities, probably over the revenues he was using for his son's education, and decided to send John to Orleans to study law. John, himself, was turning to the reformed views in religion that were already being argued in Paris, and in Orleans he definitely accepted them. His father's death allowed him to choose his own career, and he returned to Paris to become a man of letters, entering a college which was a stronghold of Humanism. At twenty-three he published a commentary on Seneca's *De Clementia* that was packed with learning, but may have been more than a mere display. Francis I was engaged at the time in persecuting Church Reformers, and Calvin under the guise of a commentary was pleading for clemency toward them. He was forced to flee from Paris in 1533 when it was discovered that he had written the address of the Rector of the University, in which Reformed views were upheld.

Calvin's exile from Paris began his life as a reformer. After wandering for a year or two with no fixed home he came to Basle and in 1536 published the *Institutes of the Christian Religion*, his best-known work as well as the clearest and most logical expression of Protestantism. Calvin took as his basis the Apostles' Creed. He devoted three parts of his book to the doctrine of the Trinity, and the fourth to the Church as the vehicle for what was to him the true Catholic, that is, the Reformed faith. Several Latin editions appeared in the next few years and a French translation, made by Calvin himself, in 1541. He travelled in Italy under an assumed name, and then decided to go to Strassburg to live. He was forced to go by way of Geneva because of warfare, and there he was persuaded to remain by Farel, the pastor of the principal church in Geneva. Calvin began lecturing on St. Paul's Epistles and attracted many townspeople to the lectures. He entered into disputation with Roman priests and astonished every one by his familiarity with the ancient Fathers of the Church, quoting accurately from memory on any subject.

Calvin proposed various reforms in the Church in Geneva, the first of which was that the "Holy Supper" should be celebrated every Lord's Day, and the whole church attend and receive. But he also placed strict regulations on the receiving of the Supper and favored excommunication for those who received unworthily. In these reforms Calvin was consciously returning to the primitive Church, where the Eucharist was the center of Church life, and was surrounded by strict regulation and discipline. His ideal was not popular, however, and finally he and Farel were exiled because they were too exacting. Calvin spent three happy years in Strassburg as pastor for French refugees from religious persecution. He was able to carry out his ideals with some success among these exiles. There he married. He was sent as a delegate to a meeting of German Protestant leaders, and voluntarily signed the Lutheran Augsburg Confession.

Affairs did not prosper in Geneva, however, and his friends there persuaded the citizens to recall Calvin and to promise to follow his ideas and teaching. The recall caused him much distress, and only after much searching of heart and urging on the part of others did he consent to return. It was the prospect of using Geneva and the

Church there as a means of spreading the reformed faith that finally persuaded him. He remained in Geneva until his death at fifty-five in 1564, but not without fierce struggles. The citizens were not really willing to follow him, and frequently he was threatened with renewed banishment. He never completely dominated the situation, for the civil Councilors, in opposition to Calvin's views, were the ecclesiastical rulers of the city. After 1555 his position was strengthened by the religious refugees from Germany.

Geneva became a shelter for those whom religious persecutions drove from their own homes, but this does not mean that complete freedom of opinion was tolerated there. The day for toleration was far off. Calvin and his associates were willing to resort to force to secure conformity in belief and practice, though of course they did so on the same ground on which all other such persecutions were conducted—the good of the community and the saving of the individual from further error. The most famous man to suffer in Geneva was Michael Servetus, who came to lecture on his new discovery of the circulation of the blood, and who ventured to express disbelief in the Trinity. He paid the penalty with his life.

In Geneva, Calvin began at once to organize schools, not only for the children but also for adults. Education was to be universal, and the backbone of the curriculum was to be religion. Calvin had no doubt that education without religion was incomplete and even dangerous. The two cardinal doctrines of Calvin, if his great system can be so summarized, were the absolute sovereignty of God and the moral responsibility of man. Educate a man with all the facts of science and literature and art, but leave these out, and Calvin saw the result would be disastrous for the individual as for society. He composed and continually revised a Catechism for the purpose, and it was said that the children of Geneva could discuss religion like "any doctor of the Sorbonne." The culmination of this educational system was to be found in the school of theology, where the pastors were to be trained by the best scholars available and sent out well able to dispute and teach the reformed faith. A sound and thoroughly educated ministry as well as laity was one of Calvin's goals, and the spread of Calvinism in Europe can be traced to the achieving of this goal.

The spread of Calvinism was also assisted by the organization Calvin provided. In Geneva the Church and the State were one, but Calvin saw that in France, for long years at least, the reformed faith would not win the whole population. Therefore he sought to provide a system for a Church that would be independent of the State. In the *Institutes* he had set forth a form of government for the Church based on what he believed to be the primitive model. Each congregation must have a threefold ministry consisting of a pastor or bishop, a body of elders and another body of deacons. The pastor was to be chosen by the others and carefully examined before being installed. In 1555 a congregation was so organized secretly in Paris, and was entirely independent of outside control. Later other congregations were organized. This was the organization for a Church in persecution. When it became possible the congregations were to be federated or organized into a national synod, called a Presbytery, or assembly of Elders, each congregation being subject to general control. This is the origin of the name Presbyterian, as the Calvinist Churches came to be called. There was a large element of democracy in this organization, more than in the primitive model perhaps, yet Calvin did not take that to mean individual liberty to accept or reject the ruling of congregation or Presbytery. Nor was there liberty in belief or practice or personal habits and morals. Calvinism was a discipline that produced character and heroism and devotion, and in this regard it followed the primitive Church. It lacked some of the joy and spontaneity of primitive Christianity, but in the Hugenots of France and in the Presbyterians of Scotland, as in the Calvinists of Switzerland and Holland, it asserted the value of the individual and the need for self-discipline.

Chapter 12

IGNATIUS LOYOLA AND THE
COUNTER REFORMATION

Ad majorem gloriam Dei

ONE THING the Lutheran and Protestant Reformation accomplished, which is often forgotten, was the reform of
the Catholic Church itself. That was what Luther desired
but could not accomplish, and the alternative for him was
revolt. But he showed churchmen that there was not only
need but also popular demand for reform, and the Counter Reformation, or Catholic Revival, was the work of
those who were determined to remain loyal to the Church
and at the same time reform it. One example of this determination was seen in Spain where, in the year Luther
nailed his theses to the castle church in Wittenberg, Francisco Ximenez, a Franciscan who was chief adviser to
Ferdinand and Isabella of Spain, and who became Archbishop of Toledo and Cardinal, began reforms both among
the clergy and in the church services. The Capuchins were
organized in 1526 as the branch of the Franciscans that
tried to follow more closely the ideals of St. Francis, and
raise the general tone of living among monks and friars.
Paul III, who became pope in 1534, began a much-needed

reform of the Papal Court by appointing to the College
of Cardinals such men as the Englishman John Fisher,
Bishop of Rochester, later beheaded by Henry VIII. St.
Teresa of Avila in Spain was a strong-minded woman who
succeeded in founding a reformed Carmelite Order for
women and persuaded her pupil, St. John of the Cross,
to found one for men.

The strongest agency, however, as well as the most
typical, in the double work of checking Protestantism by
winning back Protestants and of reforming the Church
and the papacy from within was the Society of Jesus, or the
Jesuits. This order was founded by a Spaniard known in
history as Ignatius of Loyola. His original idea was to go
to Jerusalem to care for the poor there and to convert the
Saracens, but he supplemented this purpose by saying that
he and his followers would do whatever the pope wished.
The key to the history of the Society of Jesus is to be
found in that proviso.

Ignatius, or Inigo de Recalde de Loyola, born in 1491,
was the scion of a noble or semi-noble Spanish family
which boasted that its particular corner of Spain, lying on
the Bay of Biscay at the French border, had never been
overrun by the Moors. The family moreover took pride
in possessing the privilege of a personal summons to the
coronations of the kings of Leon, and the right to send
their sons as pages to that court. Ignatius went to enter
the royal service at the court of Ferdinand of Leon, who
with his wife, Isabella of Castile, were joint patrons of
Christopher Columbus, and grandparents of Charles V,
the Holy Roman Emperor. As a boy Ignatius had some
education, and was a painter and poet of sorts. His favorite
reading was the romances of chivalry, especially the

Amadis de Gaula, the oldest and most famous of its kind.

When Ignatius was of sufficient age, he became a soldier, both to satisfy his passion for chivalry and to earn his living, since he was the eighth son, and the family fortune was none too large. He was given a place in the retinue of the Viceroy of Navarre, and he was known among his companions and by the citizens of the towns where the troops were quartered as a hot-blooded and arrogant young officer. He showed ability, however, not only as a soldier but also as a leader of men. The Viceroy in 1520 sent him to his native Basque province to try to reconcile the two factions among the noble families there, and he succeeded far beyond the Viceroy's hopes. He was a typical Basque in his careful practice of religion, but he was not distinguished from his fellows in this. Spanish soldiers of the time always before a battle confessed their sins to each other if no priest was present. Ignatius was not interested in religion save in a formal fashion. Warfare broke out between the French, who sought to control the border country, and the army of the Viceroy of Navarre. Ignatius was stationed at the fortress of Pamplona, and when his commander was ready to surrender in the face of overwhelming odds, the young officer appealed to his honor and forced a battle. Ignatius was badly wounded, his leg being shattered by a cannon ball, and, though he could not know it at the time, his career as a soldier was ended. This was in May, 1521, the year and month in which the Emperor Charles V succeeded in condemning Luther and all his works at the Diet of the Empire at Worms.

The French were sufficiently impressed with Ignatius' conduct and gallantry to allow an army surgeon to tend him, and later they sent him home on a litter as useless for further fighting and hence not worth holding as a prisoner for exchange. They were right, but only because of poor medical care. The doctor at home insisted on breaking the shattered leg again and resetting it, and then repeating the operation. A piece of bone worked its way out and made a great lump below the knee; also his leg was noticeably shorter. Ignatius insisted on having the lump sawed off, and then the leg pulled to its normal length by weights and pulleys. Somehow he lived through this ordeal, though the family had the last rites administered at the end of June. The young soldier was thinking of his graceful appearance and the looks of his leg; he succeeded with the help of the doctors merely in crippling himself hopelessly.

Ignatius was not spending the days of his convalescence in the castle of his father as he desired or planned, but those days were not thereby wasted or unproductive. He enquired for some of the much-read romances of chivalry, but found to his disgust that the castle contained only two books. These two did not interest him, a translation into Castilian of a German *Life of Christ* and a collection of *Legends of the Saints*, both pious productions of the late Middle Ages. Finally, however, boredom forced him to read them; then when he could bring himself to read them no longer, he would try to reconstruct from memory the romance of his much-loved Amadis. Memory failing him, he would return to what he had at hand. He had already realized that his military days were over. When he reached the stories about St. Francis and St. Dominic in the *Legends*, he was more interested and he began to ask himself, "What if I should become a great saint?" At the same time he carried on an interesting experiment. He took notice that whenever he thought of his lost military glory or dreamed of the lady of his chivalrous ambitions he became gloomy and depressed, but when his thoughts turned to knighthood of the cross, or when he meditated on Christ or the Blessed Virgin, he was happy and hopeful. One night he thought he saw a vision of the Virgin and her Son, and he was convinced that there was a meaning in it for him.

As soon as he was able, Ignatius determined to find out what the vision meant; he had himself hoisted on a mule and rode to the great Benedictine monastery of Montserrat, where, as any young knight would, he kept vigil before the famous statue of the Virgin. Then, without telling his family, he adopted a pilgrim's garb and started for Jerusalem. He was forced to stop at Manressa because of the plague and his own weakness, and in this delay doubt and despair filled his soul again after the first enthusiasm of his new quest had faded. He practiced all the austerities of the Church, as Luther had, and he finally came to a not dissimilar conclusion after much "travail of soul," that the sinner must throw himself on God's mercy. Ignatius did not thereby give up the austerities, however; he began rather to work out a system by which the soul could be trained to realize and feel God's love. In *The Imitation of Christ*, to which we have referred, he found the answer to his soul's search,

"The life of a good religious person ought to be mighty in all virtues; that he may inwardly be such, as outwardly he seemeth to men. . . .

"Daily ought we to renew our purpose, and to stir up ourselves to fervor, as though we had for the first time today entered the religious life, and to say, 'Help me, O My God! in this my good purpose, and in Thy holy service. . . .'

"We must diligently search into, and set in order, both the outward and the inner man" (Book I, chap. 19).

"It is a very great matter to stand in obedience, to live under a superior; and not to be at our own disposing. It is much safer to stand in subjection, than in authority" (Book I, chap. 9).

The words obedience, subjection, superior, authority—these formed the charter of the service of God for Ignatius.

Ignatius started again on his pilgrimage to Jerusalem, but on reaching there he was too anxious to lead others, and the authorities sent him home. Feeling the need of more education, and already looking to the priesthood, he began the study of Latin in the summer of 1524 at the age of thirty-three. He tried to influence others, especially students, to live more simply, and to practice the same austerities and devotion he did. This alarmed his spiritual advisers, who were nervous over heresy and new sects, and he was imprisoned for a short time and forbidden to teach or direct people in religious practices. This restriction was probably meant to end his ambitions; instead it sent him off to Paris, to study at the University. He entered the College de Montaigu in 1528, but after having influenced and reformed a wild and profligate student of the College Ste. Barbe, he obtained permission to transfer to the same college. He was admitted on the promise that he would not try to use his persuasive powers on other students, most of whom were impressionable boys compared with himself. However, he could not keep that promise, and he was nearly publicly whipped once by the masters, though he was a man forty years old.

The University of Paris was in the midst of great intellectual and theological controversy over Lutheranism and the New Learning when Ignatius came to study there. None of it seems to have bothered Ignatius, who as a military man did not question the orders of superiors. He was a Spaniard who expressed his religion in austerities, and found happiness and assurance in visions. He had by nature the ability to win the confidence of others, and then to assume responsibility for directing their religious lives. The theological arguments, or ecclesiastical abuses and their remedies, mattered to him not at all. He was concerned about the thing that seemed to him important, the direction of the spiritual life, and he travelled in France, Holland and England to study that science or art.

He soon began to win followers: Pierre Lefevre (called Peter Faber) and Francisco Javier or Xavier were among the first. They were all Spanish or Portuguese, and when with himself they numbered seven, they met to take a further step in the Church of Notre Dame on Montmartre, outside the walls of Paris, on the Feast of the Assumption (August 15), 1534. Faber, the only priest among them, said Mass, and then each one before his communion vowed to go to Jerusalem as a missionary unless the pope wished otherwise. Their first purpose was not to combat Protestantism—they seem almost not to have heard of it—nor were they founding an order. As individuals they vowed to give expression to the dream of Ignatius, the moving spirit among them. As Ignatius was ill and returning home to recuperate, they were to separate and meet in Venice in a year's time to sail to Palestine. They never sailed. Delays overtook them and finally they decided to go to Rome to ask the pope's advice. They called themselves the Company of Jesus informally, but were not organized as yet. Ignatius had suggested that they work among the sick in the hospitals, apparently with the thought (which seems modern to some) that such experience was valuable training for those who were to be ordained to the priesthood.

The pilgrimage to Palestine was abandoned at this time, and the group or Company decided on a few rules. They were to beg for their bread, travel two by two, care for the sick, and preach in the open to those who did not go to church. It sounds like a new edition of the Franciscans, or an early one of the Salvation Army. Their first preaching on street corners had as little dignity, and carried as great conviction to the ordinary man. Ironically enough they were accused of being Lutherans and suspected of heresy. The Companions agreed to separate again and meet in Rome, each one to meditate on the constitution of the Company as he travelled. Finally they laid their plans before the pope, promising to "consecrate their lives to the continual service of Christ and of the popes, and to serve the Lord and the Roman Pontiff . . . in such wise as they shall be bound to execute immediately and without hesitation or excuse all the reigning Pontiff or his successors may enjoin upon them for the profit of souls and for the propagation of the faith." Pope Paul III recognized the value in such a Company and organized them in September, 1540. Ignatius became General in 1541 and served until 1556. They began at once to reform the social evils of Rome, the hospitals, beggars and the like. They became an Order, but one that broke most of the monastic traditions. The members did not live out of the world but in it, they did not say the Daily Offices or Monastic Hours in a community, they did not wear a distinctive garb but simply that of any priest. They were a military company in a holy war, and their chief duty was obedience. The Constitution was not fully drafted until 1558, but the Company had in the principle of obedience a sufficient rule for all its activities.

Perhaps the most famous contribution made to the whole Christian Church by Ignatius was the *Spiritual Exercises,* which may well be called a drill manual of the soul. The beginning of this was in his own discovery and experience at Manressa, and in his ability to visualize his thoughts. The object was discipline; the wills of men were to be trained to respond instantly in the spiritual, as well as in the physical sphere. The method was to meditate on some incident from the life of Christ, or some teaching of the Church, some point of dogma, until one was able to visualize, until one actually saw or heard or felt the incident or subject of the meditation. The imagination was to be trained to respond, as the will of man was to respond. Ignatius said he wanted men to smell the sulphur when the subject of meditation was Hell or the punishment of the wicked. A Master of the Exercises was to train the novice in the method over a period of four weeks. The meditation was divided into four parts: the preparation by prayer, the actual subject or incident of the meditation, the definite points or heads on which to concentrate, and lastly the converse with God and accompanying resolution. This is the so-called Ignatian Method of Meditation, which many who have no first-hand knowledge of the Exercises practice, and by which they grow spiritually.

Ignatius went into great detail concerning the proper light or time of day for each meditation, the proper attitude and position to assume, whether one should have fasted or eaten. On the other hand there was to be elasticity of method and subject according to ability. The Master of the Exercises must study each novice and arrange the particular exercise for his needs. The uniqueness and perhaps lasting value of the Exercises lie in the fact that Ignatius was able to observe and codify his own experiences and reactions, and pass them on to others. If objection be made that few if any would react in the same manner, he would have pointed to the discretion allowed the Master. The simple truth is that they have proved useful to men and women everywhere to whom Catholic teaching and practice are familiar, and the method profitable to many brought up in the Evangelical tradition of "the Bible and the Bible only."

The Exercises as they stand in their entirety presupposed complete loyalty to the Church's ways and beliefs, but they were also to be the means of promoting loyalty. As we have seen, Loyola's followers were to do as they were told, absolute military obedience and discipline were their rule and life, and the pope's will or the General's will for them was the voice of God. The Exercises were the means to the end; and the reward of obedience, in thought and imagination, as well as in will, was converse and communion with God, Father, Son and Holy Ghost, or the Blessed Virgin—what the Mystics had called the Beatific Vision. Ignatius was sure however that the Vision, or the converse with God, with which each Exercise ended would send men out into the world again with fresh zeal for God's glory and the good of souls.

The Jesuit Order, as the Company of Jesus came to be known, broke with tradition in another respect. There was no woman's order. Ignatius said his company was to have nothing to do with the direction of women in the confessional, even though he had been successful in it, because it took too much time. That ideal was not strictly held, and one of the important things to notice about the Constitutions of 1558 was the insistence that nothing in them was to be considered unalterable. There was to be constant growth and the possibility of change.

The Order grew rapidly, more rapidly than Ignatius wanted, and spread to Portugal almost immediately. Spain and France were slower in taking it to themselves, but the Jesuit Colleges in Douai and Rheims in France became havens for Roman Catholics forced to flee England, especially in Elizabeth's reign. It was in these two places that the translation of the *Vulgate* into English was made for Roman Catholics, and consequently is still called the Douai or Rheims Version. The first German Jesuit was Peter Canisius who took the vows in 1549 and found his work especially among students in Cologne and later in Vienna. So influential did the Order become that two of Ignatius' original company, Lainez, who succeeded the founder as General in 1558, and Salmeron were the most influential theologians at the Council of Trent (1545–1560).

The Council of Trent, called in answer to the repeated demands made between 1526 and 1530 by the Lutherans for a general Council, so far as they were concerned, came too late. The Council was convened at three separate times in fifteen years. It unified the Roman Catholic Church by increasing the pope's power and instituting reforms among the clergy, and it so defined doctrine as to close the door on the return of Protestants unless they were willing to renounce their beliefs as errors. The Jesuits had a large hand in the Council, and were especially insistent on a better educated clergy. They also became the great exponents of a system of general education, and though there is no evidence that they had heard of Calvin's ideas, their emphasis in this regard was very similar.

In missionary work the Jesuits, along with the Franciscans and Dominicans, showed the old zeal of Christians for winning others to Christ. Francis Xavier is the best known among Jesuit missionaries. Ignatius won him in the early days in Paris with the text, "What shall it profit a man if he gain the whole world and lose his own soul?" Francis decided to save his soul by gaining the world for Christ, and in 1540 he set out for Portuguese East India. He labored for ten years in Goa, amid the appalling moral depravity of the Portuguese colony, and the childlike eagerness of the natives. Then he moved on to Japan. One of Ignatius' principles was to be "all things to all men," and Xavier decided to live as ascetic a life as Buddhist monks in Japan lived. He was at home in palace and hovel, he learned twenty languages and preached in them all. He died, hoping and trying to gain entrance to China, utterly worn out by his labors. Nowhere is his spirit better expressed then in his hymn:

> "My God, I love thee: not because
> I hope for heaven thereby;
>
> .　　　.　　　.　　　.　　　.
>
> Not with the hope of gaining aught;
> Not seeking a reward.
> But as Thyself hast lovèd me.
> O ever loving Lord."

The Jesuit missions in America are well known. Peter Claver was called a "saint in the slave trade" because he devoted his years in the West Indies to alleviating the lot of Negro slaves. Several of the Jesuit missionaries to the North American Indians were martyred, Isaac Jogues, John de Brebeuf and others. These were canonized by the Roman Catholic Church in 1930. Pere Marquette, who explored the Mississippi River as far as the entrance of the Arkansas, was a Jesuit. Franciscans and Dominicans were likewise active in all missionary work of the age, but too often they were adjuncts to the Spanish and Portuguese conquests.

Other Roman Catholic reformers of the sixteenth and early seventeenth centuries ought to be mentioned because they are so little heard of by any save members of their own Church. Philip Neri, born in 1515, sprung from aristocratic forebears, had entered a mercantile business belonging to a wealthy uncle, but he gave this up and began to study and practice charity. He was ordained in 1551 and became guide and confessor to many, especially to young men. He gathered groups of these young men around him for training in prayer and Christian living, and finally organized them into the Oratorians, so named because the hall they met in was called the Oratory. Laymen as well as priests, concerned about their spiritual life and that of the city, were included, and they combined sports and manual labor and exercise in their activities. This was a novel combination in his day, though familiar enough in ours in the Y.M.C.A. and kindred organizations. The Oratorians became a powerful influence for good.

Two other men played important parts in the Counter Reformation. St. Francis de Sales was made Bishop of Geneva in 1602, though unable to live there because the city was still the stronghold of Calvinists. He wrote an *Introduction to the Devout Life* which has had great influence on many people's prayers. Chiefly because of his virtuous life he was instrumental in restoring many Calvinists to the Church. With Madame de Chantal he founded the woman's Order of the Visitation to care for the sick poor. St. Vincent de Paul also had an interesting career. Ordained priest in 1600, he was seized by Mohammedan pirates and sold as a slave in Tunis. He converted his owner, who had been a Christian, and they escaped to France where he began preaching in French villages to combat ignorance and indifference. The group of priests who joined him were organized as Vincentians. Once he appealed to his people for food for a poor family, and got much more than could be used before it spoiled. This gave him the idea of founding an Association of

Charity, the forerunner of all Charity organizations. Sisters of Charity were organized to supervise these Associations. His work among prisoners, especially those condemned to the galleys, was also noteworthy, and King Louis XIII gave him an official position to help carry on this work.

Chapter 13

THOMAS CRANMER AND THE
REFORMATION IN ENGLAND

"Ecclesia Anglicana libera sit"

IN ENGLAND at the beginning of the sixteenth century the chief national concern was dynastic. Henry VII, who had become king in 1485 as the first Tudor sovereign, none too sure that his line was secure, had arranged a marriage between his son and heir, Prince Arthur, and Catherine of Aragon, daughter of the aristocratic Ferdinand and Isabella. Five months after the marriage was solemnized, Arthur died, at the age of sixteen. Lest he lose what had been gained, Henry persuaded the pope to allow the new heir, Prince Henry, to marry his brother's widow, though such a marriage was contrary to the Church Law. Permission was given however, and Henry married Catherine in 1509 and a few months later became King Henry VIII. The marriage turned out badly. Of the children born to Henry and Catherine, the princess Mary alone survived, and neither Henry nor the ordinary Englishman believed that a woman could govern England in those turbulent times.

For twenty years king and kingdom waited for a male heir, and then Henry began to seek some other solution. Doubts about the pope's power to allow him to marry against the Law of God were suggested to him in 1527, he said, by a French bishop who was envoy of the King of France, and made him hope the pope might agree to declare the marriage null because unlawful from the first. The biblical passage, Leviticus 20:21, which prohibited such a marriage clearly pronounced a curse of childlessness on the contracting parties, and this curse had been fulfilled. The fact that a dynastic crisis was the result strengthened the case in Henry's mind. Henry's request was not for a divorce, which he no less than the pope would have abominated, but for an annulment. The same pope had granted a similar request in the case of the King of Portugal, and almost an identical one for the Duke of Suffolk. Ordinarily the annulment would have been allowed, but the pope's hands were tied by the fact that the queen's nephew was the Emperor Charles V who, devout Catholic though he was, only waited for an excuse to attack the pope. Henry's chief agent, Cardinal Wolsey, could accomplish nothing, and he finally fell from favor. When Charles V was involved in serious dispute with the King of France, the pope sent a legate to England to try to persuade Catherine to enter a nunnery, but this was not successful either.

Unfortunately Henry's concern for a successful outcome was made more pressing by his growing infatuation for Anne Boleyn, daughter of the Earl of Wiltshire, one of his councillors. In itself this would have been of slight importance. Kings had had mistresses before, Henry himself had had; but if his queen could give him no male heir, perhaps a new queen could. The heir was the important consideration; who was queen was secondary. Events followed quickly. Henry summoned Parliament in 1529 to legislate in minor details of Church reform, but seemed not to know what to do next. Some one brought to his attention the suggestion of a Cambridge scholar, one Thomas Cranmer, that the universities of Europe be asked whether they thought the pope had power to permit the marriage in the first place. There was enough anti-papal feeling among scholars to make certain some would think not, and if the pope could not allow the marriage, his consent to dissolution and nullity was not necessary. When Henry heard of this suggestion, he cried, "That man has the sow by the right ear."

With some justice it has been said, and often repeated, that "the English Reformation produced no heroes."[1] Certainly there was no Luther, no Calvin, no Ignatius. There was none to give his name to a new Church or system, or to found a new society. But the moving spirit in the second half of Henry's reign and in that of Edward VI, the man who gave the break with Rome religious significance and made it a positive movement with a voice of its own, was the one whose suggestion on the annulment Henry was so willing to seize upon, Thomas Cranmer.

Cranmer was born not far from Sherwood Forest, in a village called Aslacton, near Nottingham. His family came from Lincolnshire and boasted a family crest, three cranes over a chevron, a play on the name, a chevron in

[1]Charles Beard, *The Reformation in Its Relation to Modern Thought* (1883), p. 305.

heraldry standing for a lake or a mere. There is a story that Henry once told him to alter the crest to "three pelicans in their piety," (*i.e.,* feeding their young on their own blood, a favorite medieval symbol), "for you are like to be tested if you stand to your tacklings." His schooling at the hands of a parish clerk was "marvellous severe and cruel," to use his own words. His father was chiefly interested in his being a good rider and huntsman, and Cranmer never lost his boyhood love and skill at these exercises. He entered Jesus College, Cambridge, and when in 1510 or 1511 he took his Bachelor's degree, he was elected a Fellow of the College. At that time Erasmus began to teach Greek in Cambridge, but there is no evidence that Cranmer came in contact with him. Nevertheless when Cranmer became archbishop he continued the pension that his predecessor, Warham, had granted Erasmus. Cranmer was, at least, a product of the New Learning. He seems not to have planned to enter the Church, for he married a relative of the mistress of the Dolphin Inn at Cambridge, and thereby lost his status as Fellow of his College since no married man could hold the position. The incident has been treated as discreditable to his career at Cambridge, and his wife called "Black Joanna, the barmaid." The marriage was no doubt a lowly one, but not necessarily dishonorable. His wife died in childbirth, however, and he was immediately re-elected to his Fellowship.

For fifteen years his life was uneventful, except that he became a priest and was known to frequent the White Horse Tavern, the center of Lutheran doctrine in Cambridge. The authorities were ever watchful lest the dons or Fellows of the colleges adopt such opinions, but Cran-

mer seems not to have been suspected. In 1530 he came
to the notice of the king through his chance suggestion to
two old Cambridge associates, Stephen Gardiner and John
Fox, both of whom were later, as bishops, to be his opponents. After this he went at the king's request to stay at
the home of the Earl of Wiltshire where he wrote for
Henry his ideas on the annulment. As Henry's special
ambassador he later went to Rome and to Germany. In
Germany, though a priest, he married the niece of Osian-
der, a theologian and reformer. Their marriage no doubt
indicates Cranmer's break with the old order, but it was
a bold step for one who enjoyed Henry's favor, for the
king would not approve it. In fact the marriage caused him
considerable uneasiness when in 1532 he was summoned
home to become Archbishop of Canterbury.

The appointment was a surprise to all, to none so much
as to Cranmer himself. He delayed returning for several
months hoping the king would reconsider. The clergy in
Convocation the year previous had followed Archbishop
Warham in recognizing Henry as "the only and supreme
lord, and so far as the law of Christ permits, the supreme
head" of the Church of England. The pope, choosing to
ignore this action, and acting apparently on Henry's suggestion, issued the proper documents for Cranmer's consecration in order to lose none of the revenues which
would go to the king until a new archbishop was installed.
Before Cranmer was consecrated on March 30, 1533, he
drew up a document maintaining that he would consider
his oath of allegiance to the pope binding only so far as it
did not conflict with his prior loyalty to the king. Bishops,
without so stating it in the past, had so acted, and to Cran-

mer must go credit for candor. He accepted the royal supremacy as a settled fact in England when he became archbishop. Moreover he had returned to scripture, as Wycliffe and Erasmus advocated, and he found there that submission to the civil power was expressly enjoined and no exception was made in spiritual matters, nor was the pope's authority so much as mentioned.

Cranmer can hardly be accused of delay in the most pressing business before him as archbishop. Immediately after his consecration he constituted his ecclesiastical court and decreed the marriage with Catherine null and void, because manifestly contrary to the law of God, and the marriage of Henry and Anne Boleyn, already solemnized on January 25 of the same year, a valid and lawful union. This was the immediate purpose for which he had been chosen, and he proved himself a pliant enough prelate for Henry or for any prince. On June 1 the new queen was crowned in Westminster Abbey; three months later the future Queen Elizabeth was born, and still there was no male heir.

In 1534 Henry persuaded Parliament to pass the Act of Supremacy proclaiming the king "Supreme Head in earth of the Church and clergy of England," with no mention of the clause the clergy had inserted two years before, "so far as the law of Christ allows." This Act brought the resignation of the Lord Chancellor, Sir Thomas More, "the King's servant but God's first," and in the end it was refusal to accept the king's supremacy, even tacitly, which brought More to the headsman's block. John Fisher, bishop of Rochester, and Cardinal, suffered the same fate for a like refusal. The story of these two makes as fair a page as any history can produce. Parliament so little understood the Act of Supremacy that it also forbade by specific acts any appeal to the pope, and the payment of "Peter's price" or of annates, *i.e.*, the income of the first year paid the pope by all bishops on receipt of his confirmation of their appointment. To minds less astute than Sir Thomas More's, even to Henry's mind perhaps, the Supremacy reasserted only what the kings of England had tried to maintain, with varying success, since William the Conqueror.

Henry made it clear that he was not repudiating Catholic doctrine. As second son, and not the heir to the throne, Henry had received a good education, even some theology, and had probably been destined for the Church. He still stood by the refutation he wrote of Luther's theses in 1518, and for which he had received from the pope the new title "Defensor Fidei," a title still used by the kings of England. He retained all the rites and ceremonies of the Church, and burned as heretics those who professed Protestant doctrines. He was anti-papal for practical reasons, as were many Englishmen, but he was not anti-Catholic. The last thing Henry intended to do was found a new Church; it was the old Church of England with its allegiance to the king over the pope, so long implicit, made explicit. Convocation soon reaffirmed the Papal Supremacy with a new declaration, "the Bishop of Rome hath no more authority in this kingdom than any other foreign bishop." Cranmer was prepared to go further than Henry, but even he did not believe the king was founding a new Church.

Cranmer's relations with Henry remained cordial, even

intimate, though the two were in real disagreement over matters of doctrine and practice. The archbishop disapproved of the famous Six Articles which Henry published in 1539, by which transubstantiation was affirmed, communion in one kind (the bread only, as is the Roman Catholic practice today) for the laity was ordered, confessions made obligatory, and clerical marriages forbidden. Henry seems not to have cared what Cranmer thought so long as he taught nothing contrary to the Catholic faith. Cranmer was willing to keep silent, even to compromise in a way Luther or Loyola could never have done, because he was patiently working and planning for the future. He was not concerning himself over doctrine, but he was busy with other things.

During Henry's reign he accomplished one of his goals, an authorized translation of the Bible in English. One had been made, though incomplete, from Greek and Hebrew, in 1526 by William Tyndale, an exiled English scholar in Holland, and this had been smuggled into England. Cranmer agreed heartily with Tyndale's avowed purpose. "If God spare my life I will, ere many years, cause the boy that driveth the plough to know more scripture than the ordinary priest doth." His translation was condemned by Henry however. Cranmer therefore persuaded Henry to approve a version made in 1535 from the Latin Vulgate by Miles Coverdale, later to become Bishop of Exeter. In 1537 one John Rogers, using the pseudonym, "Thomas Matthew," reprinted Tyndale's, filling in the gaps with Coverdale's. This version, revised in 1538 with a preface by Cranmer, and so called Cranmer's or the Great Bible, was ordered set up in every parish church in the kingdom in order that people might read it. The Psalms in the *Book of Common Prayer* are from this version. Gardiner, Bishop of Winchester, Cranmer's old friend and now his opponent, tried to have a translation authorized which left all the controversial words in Latin but he was prevented by the archbishop. Cranmer's words in the preface to the Great Bible express his own use of scripture: "Every man that cometh to the reading of this Holy Book ought to bring with him first and foremost the fear of Almighty God, and next a firm and stable purpose to reform his own self according there unto; and so to continue, proceed and prosper, from time to time showing himself to be a sober and fruitful hearer and learner."

Cranmer had enemies who were always seeking to destroy him, but the king continued his protector. On one occasion the Canons, or clergy, of Canterbury Cathedral accused him to Henry of being heretical. The king summoned his archbishop saying, "Now I know who is the greatest heretic in Kent," and then told Cranmer to investigate the charge himself. The King's Council once decided to commit the archbishop to the Tower while investigating his actions and beliefs. Henry warned Cranmer and gave him the royal signet ring to use if an appeal to the king was necessary. The Council summoned Cranmer, kept him waiting several hours in the anteroom, then summarily ordered him to the Tower. He produced the ring, and the Council, like schoolboys, went at once to Henry, who rebuked them for their discourtesy in keeping Cranmer waiting, and then turned to other matters in which he particularly deferred to the archbishop's opinions. It was Cranmer who held Henry's hand as the king lay dying, and Henry pressed it gently when he could no longer speak.

Edward VI, a boy of nine when he came to the throne in 1547, on the death of Henry, was Henry's only male heir, the son of Jane Seymour, his father's third wife. Anne Boleyn had been executed as unfaithful to Henry though she solemnly denied it to the end. Cranmer was one of the few who pled for mercy for Anne, as he later pled for the lives of More and Fisher, but he found ground for annulment of the marriage of Anne and Henry. Edward ruled through a Council of Regency appointed by Henry before his death. Cranmer was a member of the Council, but he appears to have taken little part in its proceedings. He was again busy on matters of church business. The opportunity which had been denied him in Henry's reign had come. This was the preparation and publication of his greatest contribution to religion, not simply to the Church and realm of England, the *Book of Common Prayer*. The primary aim of the Book was expressed in Cranmer's preface: to restore the Bible to its primary place in worship, to return to the ancient custom, "enjoined by St. Paul," of services in the language of the people, to simplify the services and include all in the compass of one volume, and to secure uniformity throughout England. The book was essentially the people's book, "Common Prayer," and the daily services, based on the Monastic Hours, were reduced to two, Morning and Evening Prayer.

Cranmer's gift for translating and formulating devotional prose in English is comparable to St. Augustine's

ability to use Latin. It was not the gift that Henry valued
however. In 1545 the king had allowed a Primer, or book
of private prayers, in English for the layman's use; but
permission was probably won because of a petition in the
Litany, forerunner of the Prayer Book Litany, which ran
"From all sedition and privy conspiracy, from the tyranny
of the Bishop of Rome and all his detestable enormities,
from all false doctrine and heresy . . . *Good Lord, de-
liver us.*" This petition appeared in the two Prayer Books
of Edward's reign, but disappeared in that of Elizabeth.
The genius of Cranmer's writing lies in his rhythm and
his ability to express timeless ideas in the language of
the time in which he lived. For example, he took his material from all the Latin sources at his disposal, among
others, the Sacramentary or Mass Book of Pope Gelasius
(*c.* 500 A.D.). The Dark Ages were, as we have seen, times
of great personal insecurity, and that is reflected in the
Sacramentary. Cranmer took some of them, familiar in
Latin to generations of English monks and clergy, and expressed the insecurity of the Tudor age, as of later ages,
in English that will never die. "Give unto thy servants that
peace which the world cannot give; that both our hearts
may be set to obey thy commandments, and also that by
thee we being defended from the fear of our enemies may
pass our time in rest and quietness." "Lighten our darkness, we beseech thee, O Lord; and by thy great mercy
defend us from all perils and dangers of this night."

Two prayer books were issued in Edward's reign, the
first in 1549, the second in 1552. The second book moved
noticeably in a Reformed direction, doubtless as Cranmer
did. He wrote so much that it is not always possible to tell

how far he had moved; moreover he had all the caution of a scholar and the desire to weigh every definition. The clearest indication of the movement toward the Reformed ideas, however, is to be seen in the central service of the two books. In the first book that service was called, "The Supper of the Lord or the Holy Communion, commonly called the Mass," in the second more simply, "The Supper of the Lord or the Holy Communion." The first Book ordered the traditional Mass Vestments to be used, the second made no mention of vestments. The first Book provided that the priest say at the distribution of the Sacrament, "The Body (or Blood) of our Lord Jesus Christ which was given (or shed) for thee, preserve thy body and soul unto everlasting life"; the second substituted, "Take and eat this in remembrance that Christ died for thee, and feed on him in thy heart by faith with thanksgiving," and "Drink this in remembrance that Christ's blood was shed for thee, and be thankful." Cranmer had definitely rejected transubstantiation, and yet he wrote, "I do not say that Christ's Body and Blood be given in signification and not in deed. But I do plainly speak that Christ's Body and Blood be given us indeed, not carnally and corporally, but spiritually and effectually."[2] The best summary of his views perhaps is to be found by combining the two sentences of administration, as was done in the Elizabethan Book and in all subsequent ones. Before the English Prayer Books, and for centuries, the people had consistently neglected even the one Communion expected of them each year. Cranmer, through the Books of Common

[2]"On the Lord's Supper" in the Parker Society Edition of *Cranmer's Works*, p. 37.

Prayer, succeeded in his ambition to "restore the communion to the people."

The Injunctions of 1547, the first year of Edward's
reign, reveal Cranmer's further aims for the Church of
England. One sermon was to be preached every quarter
in every parish church, an order which reveals much about
preaching in England before the Reformation. The Creed,
the Lord's Prayer, and the Ten Commandments were to
be learned by the people in English, the sacraments were
to be duly administered, a Bible was to be placed in every
parish church, together with the Paraphrases of Erasmus,
and the Epistle and Gospel at Mass were to be read or
sung in English. In a footnote to a treatise, "Of ceremonies, why some be abolished and some retained," which
Cranmer placed at the end of the first Prayer Book, he
said, "As touching kneeling, crossing (oneself) . . . and
other gestures, they may be used or left as every man's
devotion serveth."

Edward died in 1553 and Mary Tudor became queen
amid great rejoicing. People had had enough of the Re-
gent Northumberland and his machinations. Spurred on
by her Spanish husband, Philip II, Mary turned at once
to the religious situation. Her marriage had lost her some
popularity, the treatment she accorded the archbishop and
others, by which she won the title "Bloody Mary," lost
all the rest. Mary had a personal grudge against Cranmer
who had pronounced her mother's marriage no marriage,
and she had him arrested at once. She was also astute
enough to see the opportunity that presented itself to pro-
mote through him the ecclesiastical settlement she desired.
Cranmer, she knew, was in a real dilemma. He had always

held that a man's first duty was to his sovereign and his sovereign's beliefs, whatever he himself might think or believe. Hence he remained at his post when the Six Articles were in force. Henry, knowing Cranmer's opinions, was willing that he should say nothing and do nothing toward enforcing them. Mary, also knowing Cranmer's opinions, was determined to make him speak. Whether he recanted his reformed views, as his idea of the supremacy demanded, or refused to recant, and so repudiated the supremacy, either way he would discredit his own cause. Some one has suggested that a modern Roman Catholic would find himself in the same dilemma if the pope should suddenly turn Protestant.

True to his convictions, Cranmer recanted not once nor twice but seven times, each time signing a more abject document than before. His examiners used the form of torture that would hurt him most when they kept demanding a new recantation. All this he did at the queen's word, and it may be to save his life, though after the burning of Latimer and Ridley, two of Cranmer's friends and supporters, he must have known there was scant hope of that. On March 21, 1556, he was taken to St. Mary's Church, Oxford, to hear a Sermon, and afterward to read his latest submission to the queen's will and to the pope's authority. When he stood up to read, it is not clear that he knew he was to be burned, but all went well as long as he kept to the document before him. Suddenly, however, he took a new line,

"And now I come to the great thing that so troubleth my conscience, more than anything that I said or did in my life; and that is my setting abroad of writings contrary to the truth, which here I now renounce and refuse as things written with my hand contrary to the truth which I thought in my heart, [Thus far there was nothing in this to disturb his judges, but then] and written for fear of death, and to save my life, if it may be: and that is all such bills that I have written or signed with my own hand since my degradation; wherein I have written many things untrue. And forasmuch as my hand offended contrary to my heart, if I come to the fire, it shall be first."[3]

He was dragged out before he could say more, and once on his way, he ran so fast that his warders could scarcely keep up with him. He kept his word, too, about thrusting his right hand first into the flames. He and Sir Thomas More, whom the Church now calls St. Thomas More, reached at the last the same position, that a man's conscience must make the final decision.

The English Reformation produced no heroes; but it was not without its deeds of heroism, nor was it without solid accomplishments and results. Primarily Cranmer was a scholar who perhaps ought to have been left in his study. He was not a prophet nor a strong man, but of little use would a strong man have been in Henry's reign or in the Council of Regency dominated by the Duke of Northumberland. We may disagree with his ideas of the royal supremacy, and deprecate his part in the marriage of Henry and Anne Boleyn. We may mourn his mistakes and seeming lack of courage, though we cannot forget the final scene of his life. His personal disinterestedness, in a day when churchmen worked for their own private ends and fortunes, gives us a new measure of his character; he is said never to have asked a single favor for any member

[3]Cited in A. F. Pollard, *Thomas Cranmer*, p. 381.

of his family. His one ambition was, as he put it in a letter to Thomas Cromwell in 1535, to be, *"apostolos Jesu Christi . . .* so that the very Christian conversation (*i.e.,* the daily life) of the people might be the seals of our office." The true index to his inner life is to be found in his devotional prose; and his gifts of the English Prayer Books and a worthy translation of the Bible have placed all English-speaking Christians in eternal debt to him.

When Elizabeth came to the throne in 1558, after Mary's death, the religious question had been settled. It remained only for her to give it expression. Mary, by her zeal for Rome and by her Spanish marriage, had made it impossible for England to return to the Roman obedience. The pope is said to have offered to recognize Elizabeth as the rightful queen if she would acknowledge his supremacy. The daughter of Anne Boleyn, who boasted in Tudor fashion that she was "mere English," and not, as her half-sister Mary, the daughter of a foreign princess, knew what her subjects would wish. She was crowned queen in Westminster Abbey by the Bishop of Carlyle, who used the Latin service. The Act of Uniformity restored the second Prayer Book of Edward, but permitted the vestments in use "by the authority of Parliament in the second year of Edward VI," and combined the two sentences of administration. The Act of Supremacy proclaimed Elizabeth "Supreme Governor of this realm in all spiritual or ecclesiastical things or causes," and set up Ecclesiastical Commissioners to exercise the authority thus proclaimed. Reginald Pole, Mary's archbishop, had died the same day as Mary, and Matthew Parker was chosen to fill that office. Parker had once been Elizabeth's tutor, Master of a Cambridge College and Dean of Lincoln. As a married priest he had been deprived of his living and offices by Mary, but unharmed. He was consecrated by four bishops, two of whom had been consecrated with the Latin rites in Henry's reign, and two in Edward's by the English Ordinal. Parker was the first archbishop to receive no papal approval and to seek none.

The two Acts and the consecration of Parker formed the Elizabethan Settlement which in practice still obtains in England. The Church is "by law established," the Crown holding the appointive power which today is exercised in this as in other matters by Parliament and the Prime Minister. The king's power is in no sense priestly or episcopal, it is administrative and judicial only. Elizabeth was excommunicated by the pope in 1570 after she had been queen for twelve years; Englishmen should then have refused to acknowledge her, but few, even among Roman Catholics, did refuse. Nor did many of the clergy find reason for forsaking their work, or withdrawing from the Church. What persecution there was under Elizabeth came as a result of political attempts to overthrow the queen and not for religious reasons. Mary, Queen of Scots, suffered because she was the nearest claimant to the throne and the center of the plots against Elizabeth.

There were on the other hand many extreme Protestants in England who felt that reform had not gone far enough. They wanted to abolish bishops, the Prayer Book, vestments and all such. Those who refused to accept the settlement were called Non-conformists or Dissenters, and in 1543 some of these fled to Holland, and later to New

England as the Pilgrims. Some stayed within the Church and agitated for reform; these are the Puritans, though the meaning of the word is often misunderstood. Elizabeth's successor, James VI of Scotland, son of Mary, Queen of Scots, who himself was no Catholic, called Puritans and the bishops together in the Hampton Court Conference. Only one constructive result came of this conference, namely, a new translation of the Bible, known as the King James or Authorized Version of 1611, made from the original tongues, but which followed nevertheless many turns of expression used by Wycliffe and Tyndale.

The seventeenth century was a period of violent reaction to the Elizabethan Settlement on the part of Puritans, and equally violent determination on the part of Anglicans, as members of the Established Church came to be called, to maintain the *status quo*. Coupled with this was another problem inherited from the Tudors, that of the Divine Right of Kings. The century produced many great men, religious leaders as well as others, but they failed to bring peace and understanding to their times. None of them had learned tolerance for another's views, and therein may lie the reason for their failure. Toleration was first made a working principle in America, in the Providence Plantations by Roger Williams, in Maryland under the Lords Baltimore, and in Pennsylvania under William Penn. Williams was a Baptist, the Lords Baltimore were Catholics, and Penn a Quaker, and, unfortunately, the growth of tolerance carried with it a growth in the divisions in Christianity. The history of Christianity becomes consequently more complicated from now on. It is not enough to say of a man that he is a Christian; we have now to say what kind of Christian, what "denomination," as the phrase goes. It is just these denominational divisions which present one of the problems to be solved by Christians of this and coming generations.

Chapter 14

JOHN WESLEY

"The world is my parish"

GEORGE I, of the German house of Hanover, great-grand-son of James I, became king of England in 1714. With him a new era began in English history. He could speak no English and hence was forced to depend on his Prime Minister. Thus arose the present English system of Parliamentary government. Sir Robert Walpole, the most noted of the early Prime Ministers, has doubtless been painted blacker than he actually was, but he did not hesitate to employ bribery to further his ends. Greater than he among Prime Ministers perhaps were Charles James Fox and William Pitt. Before the century had run its course, the American colonies had been lost to Britain, but the Indian Empire had been won. Laws against Dissenters were in force throughout the period, forbidding their holding office or entering the two Universities of Oxford and Cambridge. The franchise was denied those not meeting property qualifications.

The Enclosure Acts worked great hardship on the villagers, who depended on the common lands for their tillage and pasturage, and were thus deprived of all means of livelihood. Goldsmith's *The Deserted Village* pictures such a situation; the villagers crowded into the large towns and poor relief became necessary in growing volume. The Poor Laws, inherited from Elizabeth's day when it could be assumed that idleness and unemployment were willful, were out of date. The invention of the spinning jenny and the use of steam took up some of this slack population, but industry brought its own problem: child labor in great numbers, no protection for workers, and other problems. A great chasm existed between the upper and lower classes, with employers feeling no responsibility for their workers. Wages averaged from sixty to ninety cents a week, and hunger and want drove many to crime.

Prison conditions were unspeakable. There was no effort to provide drainage, food, or beds; nor was there any segregation of men and women, of hardened criminals and first offenders, of prisoners for debt and desperados. Society at large felt no concern about these things. Two men stand out because of their efforts in these regards when most men were apathetic. John Howard published an exhaustive study of prisons in England and on the Continent, and made recommendations for reform. General James Oglethorpe secured land south of the Savannah River, which he called Georgia, to plant a colony of carefully picked prisoners as well as to supply a refuge for persecuted religious minorities from Germany. The criminal code in England was severe; yet crime abounded. Coaches out of London were continually being held up by highwaymen, of whom Dick Turpin was the most famous. Assaults and robberies were frequent in London in broad daylight. The death penalty was possible for stealing a horse or a sheep, or any article worth more than five shillings, or picking a man's pocket of more than twelve pence, and thus to the number of one hundred and sixty offenses. Until 1790 a woman who killed her husband was burned at the stake. The public hangings in Tyburn were spectacles to which the whole family was taken.

Drunkenness was prevalent among all classes, so much so that one historian[1] considered it the most serious evil of the times, "incomparably more so than any event in the purely political or military annals of the century." In the grog shops, which abounded in London, the poor were invited to get drunk for a penny, dead drunk for twopence, and straw was provided for them to sleep the night on the floor. Doctor Johnson once said that in his youth "all the decent people of Lichfield got drunk every night and were not the less thought of." Violent epidemics swept through the cities, chief among them cholera and smallpox. Lady Mary Montague, whose husband was minister to Turkey, found the Turks using an inoculation against smallpox which she brought back to England, but few Englishmen would allow its use on them.

In literature the age opened brilliantly though its poetry was highly artificial and even "prosaic." The great names include Alexander Pope, Joseph Addison, Jonathan Swift, Richard Steele, Daniel Defoe, Oliver Goldsmith, Richard Brinsley Sheridan, and above all Doctor Samuel Johnson. Music was dominated by Händel, the German composer of the *Messiah* with its *Hallelujah Chorus* and

[1]W. E. H. Lecky, *England in the Eighteenth Century*, Vol. I, p. 519.

numerous other works, who spent much of his life in England. Italian opera had a great vogue, to the disgust of Doctor Johnson. On the stage were David Garrick and Mrs. Siddons. In painting, Hogarth, Gainsborough, Sir Joshua Reynolds, and Romney were supreme. The age is still famous for Wedgwood pottery, and the furniture of Chippendale, Sheraton, and Hepplewhite.

In religion things were in a poor state. The Vicar of Wakefield was typical of many a country parson who tried to inculcate homely virtues, and undoubtedly he often succeeded. But as often he joined hands with the squire to keep things as they were, and neglected the people's misery. Many of the clergy were younger sons who accepted the revenues of the parish without doing any of the work or going near their posts, and hiring curates to hold occasional services for them. Bishops did not feel any necessity for visiting their dioceses, and pluralism was as common as it had been in the Middle Ages. John Bunyan, in the previous century, had said from jail that those who cared most for the spirit of prayer were to be found in prison and those who cared most for the form of prayer in the ale houses. Among the fashionable, a visiting Frenchman reported, "every one laughs if he talks of religion." Bishop Butler wrote, "the deplorable distinction of our age is an avowed scorn of religion and a growing disregard of it." This same Bishop Butler wrote a learned work, the *Analogy of Religion*, to prove that Christianity was "reasonable," and the book is a great philosophical work. But it had no effect on the mass of Englishmen. Thomas Carlyle summed up the century tersely, "Soul extinct, stomach well alive."

Into this century John Wesley was born in 1703, of a family that had famous connections, seven generations of them appearing in the *Dictionary of National Biography*. Wesley's father, a friend of Pope and Swift and Dryden, was a sharp tongued country clergyman, rector of Epworth in Lincolnshire, strict with his family and parishioners. His mother, Susannah, was a woman of rare gifts; the daughter of a Dissenting minister, she read Greek and Latin and French in her father's library, and decided to join the Established Church. At nineteen she married Samuel Wesley, and she managed not only the household but also the parish thereafter, while he wrote verse or dug in his loved garden. Her children, nineteen in all, were taught to read by her at an early age, with the Bible as a textbook, in Greek as well as in English. When her husband was in prison for debt, she conducted meetings for worship in the barn which were better attended than his in the church, and for this he rebuked her. The rectory burned to the ground, having been set on fire by spiteful parishioners, when John was six, and in the confusion of getting the family out he was forgotten until the count was taken. Then it was too late to go in after him. His face appeared at a window, and by forming a pyramid the neighbors rescued him just as the window fell in. His mother called him from that time "a brand plucked from the burning" and felt a premonition that he was destined to great things.

At ten John went to the Charterhouse School in London, where his only recreations were reading Hebrew and running three times around the schoolhouse yard before breakfast. At seventeen he entered Christ Church, Oxford, a very different place from the Oxford of today. Edward Gibbon, the historian, who entered in 1752, tells us that professors had given up any pretense of teaching, and students drank and gambled and neglected all study. Indifference to scholarship, morals, and religion was the rule. Only members of the Established Church were admitted though no attention was paid to religious life or instruction. Wesley was described as "a very sensible active collegian . . . of finest classical talents, of most liberal and manly sentiments, gay and sprightly, with a turn to wit and humor." He kept up the practice of religion which he had learned at home, and began to consider seriously his prayers and Communions and to read religious books. In a long correspondence with his mother on the subject he came to his decision to be ordained, and he was made a deacon in 1725. A year later he was elected a Fellow of Lincoln College, with a small salary and light duties, though he became a hard worker himself. This Fellowship he ever considered his highest honor and in after years always placed on the title page of the books he wrote, "John Wesley, M.A., Sometime Fellow of Lincoln College, Oxford."

In 1727 he returned home to assist his father, but with small success. He could not adapt himself or be friendly with the parishioners, he was too self-centered in his religious life. In 1729 he returned to Oxford and, with his brother Charles and other friends, he founded a club which met daily to read the classics on weekdays and the Greek Testament on Sundays, pledged themselves to go regularly to Holy Communion and to arrange their days systematically, to review their conduct often, to live simply, and to visit the prisoners in the jail and the poor in the workhouses. They were unquestionably self-conscious, and perhaps self-righteous, and they were dubbed "Methodists" in scorn by others because of their system and regularity.

In 1735 Wesley's father died, and he was urged to apply for the parish. Instead he accepted an invitation from General Oglethorpe, and went out to Georgia with his brother Charles. He had hoped to try to convert the Indians, but he was persuaded to stay in Savannah. Again he failed. He was dictatorial and tactless, and finally had to give up his efforts. In December, 1737, he started home with bitter disappointment in his heart. "I went to Georgia to convert the Indians, but who shall convert me?" On the voyage to America he had met some German refugees who belonged to a sect called Moravians; to converse with them he had learned German, and he was much impressed with the depth of their religious life. Back in London he made the friendship of other Moravians and, in his despair, one of them advised him to forget his failures and start afresh. This came as a new revelation to him. In a meeting in Aldersgate Street, whether of the Moravians or of a society of the Church is a matter of dispute, he heard some one read from Luther's *Preface to the Epistle to the Romans* and he wrote, "I felt my heart strangely moved. I felt I did believe in Christ." He went to Germany to see more of the Moravians, and on returning preached with enthusiasm, and straightway got into trouble with the Church authorities because of this breach of good taste. Parish churches were closed to him, and he turned to the wretched debtors in prison.

George Whitefield, who had been a member of the Oxford Club, was becoming more and more interested in work among the poor. He, too, had been in Georgia, and had founded an orphanage there. He was no scholar but he was a great orator. In Gloucester Cathedral his preaching was reported to have driven some people mad, to which report the bishop replied that he hoped the madness would last until the next Sunday. In London he had drawn great crowds but had been shut out of the churches; then he went to the Bristol collieries and began to preach to the miners at the coal pits. He invited Wesley to join him, but Wesley's aristocratic soul drew back from such a breaking of the proprieties. "All my life till very lately I have been so tenacious of every point relating to decency and order that I should have thought the saving of souls almost a sin if it were not done in a church." But the argument from the fact which Whitefield presented was compelling to him. "I submitted to be even yet more vile, and proclaimed in the highways the glad tidings of salvation." After April 1, 1731, Wesley himself took to "field preaching," and the practice probably saved his life, for it kept him out of doors; he had been declared tubercular and given but a few years to live. He never weighed more than one hundred and twenty pounds, and was only five feet five inches tall.

The two Wesleys and Whitefield now began their travelling and preaching that swept England and Wales like wildfire and stirred to life the religious enthusiasm of men and women. They preached to crowds wherever a crowd would gather, and then sought to preserve the good effects by forming "societies" which were to be at-

tached to the parish churches. These societies were carefully organized by Wesley; first in order to raise money
for the poor in Bristol and then to conserve the fruits of
the religious revival. But in most cases this was done without the blessing of the parish clergy. Members of the societies were therefore often refused the Holy Communion
and otherwise persecuted. Wesley was forced to build
meeting houses and register them as Dissenters to comply
with the law, and finally to permit the leaders to celebrate
the Communion where it was impossible to receive it in the
parish church. The first "Conference," consisting of six
clergymen and four laymen, was held in 1744. Plans were
laid at once for schools and orphanages. He started a
school at Kingswood but would take pupils only from parents who would give their children entirely to the school
without taking them away 'even for a day.' The children
themselves were wakened at four winter and summer, and
fasted until three on Fridays. There were to be no play-
times and no holidays.

At this time Wesley himself began his extraordinary
record of travel and activity. In fifty years he averaged
4500 miles a year on horseback, and preached as often as
three times a day. He said that he simplified his style by
preaching to an old maid servant and cutting out all she
could not understand. His daily schedule consisted of rising at four o'clock, reading and praying until five, preaching to people who went to work at half past six; breakfast
over at seven he rode on and read as he rode, stopping
when a hard passage forced it. At noon he would preach
in a churchyard or public square, ride on afterwards to
preach again at five and sometimes to preach or to hold

a meeting after supper. He was probably the best read man in England, and he wrote and published low-priced books for his local preachers on every conceivable subject; grammar, logic, history, medicine, politics, poetry. Moreover the Journal of his daily life runs into seven hundred thousand words.

Dangerous opposition soon arose; the parish clergy even hired ruffians to pelt him with stones and beat him, and often he suffered bodily violence. Through all these difficulties he never lost courage or serenity. He continued to preach a gospel of God's love and care for individuals; there was no "hell and damnation" in his preaching. His Journal tells in simple words of his persistence in spite of violent opposition:

"October, 1743. Two years ago a piece of brick grazed my shoulder. It was a year after that that the stone struck me between the eyes. Last month I received one blow and this evening two—but both were as nothing!"

"October, 1749. We came to Bolton about five this evening—such rage and bitterness I scarcely ever saw before in any creatures that bore the form of men. They followed me in full cry—my heart was filled with love, my eyes with tears and my mouth with arguments. They were amazed, they were ashamed, they were melted down, they devoured every word."

Slowly and without his consent his societies, particularly in America, were forced to separate from the Church of England. To shepherd the flock there he tried to have two men ordained, but no bishop would have anything to do with him. In desperation he finally "set them apart" himself, having been persuaded that in the New Testament ordination was not always reserved to bishops. In

1784 he sent Thomas Coke to be "superintendent" for the work in America. On his arrival there Coke began to call himself a "bishop." Wesley wrote him in no uncertain terms, "How can you, how dare you suffer yourself to be called Bishop? I shudder, I start at the very thought." He himself died as a priest of the Church of England.

Wesley's married life was not happy. Twice his brother Charles prevented him from marrying, once in Georgia and once in London, but he finally married a London widow who was not sympathetic with him or his work. She was jealous, and he inconsiderate or engrossed in other things. In a tract on marriage he betrayed his own experience when he wrote that a wife's duties were twofold: to recognize herself the inferior of her husband and to behave as such.

His large royalties from his books, amounting perhaps to $150,000, went to take care of the poor and to further his work, and he died "leaving behind him nothing but a good library of books, a well worn clergyman's gown, a much abused reputation and—the Methodist Church." He was a scholar and loved intellectual pursuits; throughout his life he carried on his correspondence with his brother Charles in Latin.

He has been compared to Ignatius Loyola as an organizer, and it is certain that he allowed no one to interfere with his command. He held his preachers responsible for their personal character as well as for the result of their labors, but he asked no one to do what he did not do himself and, behind his rule, his love was known and recognized by all. Doctor Samuel Johnson bears witness to his charm. "I hate to meet John Wesley; the dog enchants you with his conversation, and then breaks away to go and visit some old woman. . . . He is always obliged to go at a certain hour. This is very disagreeable to a man who loves to fold his legs and have his talk out as I do."

In his zeal to help the neglected people in England, and to arouse religious men, he was not intolerant. "I have no more right to object to a man for holding a different opinion from mine than I have to differ with a man because he wears a wig and I wear my own hair." "Is thy heart as my heart? Then give me thine hand," he would quote from the Old Testament (II Kings, 10:15). "The thing which I resolved to use every possible method of preventing was a narrowness of spirit, a party zeal . . . that miserable bigotry which makes men so unready to believe that there is any work of God but among themselves." When his nephew, Charles' son, entered the Roman Catholic Church, his father could not be reconciled, but John wrote "Sammy": "whether of this church or that, I care not . . . except ye be born again ye cannot see the Kingdom of God."

The man who failed in an obscure parish in England and again in a pioneer community in Georgia turned his failure into a signal success in England and the world. How? He would have said that it was possible only as he moved out of his formal and constricted religious practices, and entered fully into the realization that as a son of God his first duty, after that he owed to God, was not to his own spiritual cultivation but to his fellow men. "The Bible knows nothing of solitary religion" was the way he put it. He took long years in making the discovery and then only at the cost of bitter personal failure, but it became the emphasis of his life henceforth and the secret of all his activity. He spoke of the "straight way of the religion of love" and of finding "that love of God and of all mankind which he had elsewhere sought in vain. No scripture can mean that God is not love." This faith he had worked out in his own experience, but he found his experience wonderfully corroborated in the Gospels. He had worked back to the emphasis he found there, and his center was ever the love of God as revealed in Christ.

The contributions of such a man are summed up with difficulty. He revived the religious life of England. The Methodists who separated from the Established Church were a mighty religious force, and the Evangelical Party, consisting of Wesley's followers who stayed in the Church, were no less mighty. What was written of England at the beginning of the eighteenth century could not be written of England at the close, and this was almost wholly the result of Wesley's work. Lecky the historian writes, "It is no exaggeration to say that he has had a wider constructive influence in the sphere of practical religion than any other man who has appeared since the sixteenth century . . . [his preaching was] of greater historic importance than all the splendid victories by land and sea won under Pitt."[2] The hymns which he and his brother Charles wrote and translated set the Methodist movement singing, and added much to the religious poetry of the English language.

He was as mighty in social and educational reforms. The last letter he wrote before his death was to William Wilberforce, urging him on in his fight to destroy the

[2]W. E. H. Lecky, *England in the Eighteenth Century*, Vol. II, p. 687.

slave trade. Sunday school, orphanages and other social agencies, even those founded by others, owe much of their inspiration to his work. He himself scarcely realized the tremendous social and industrial changes which were going on, and which were to cry out for the concern of religious men in a few years. But his work among the neglected and despised coal miners opened up the way for social work all along the line, and men like Wilberforce and Shaftesbury, the latter unconsciously perhaps, were following in his train. It has been said that he saved England from the horrors of the French Revolution by changing many of the conditions which might have brought revolution, and in that sense he remade society. Largely because of the Methodist movement the British Labor Party has never been anti-Christian, as have nearly all European Labor movements.

Chapter 15

"HOLY AND HUMBLE
MEN OF HEART"

THE NINETEENTH CENTURY was marked by great industrial and scientific advance, and consequently was a period
of great social readjustment. The century was also marked
among Christians by deep concern for tasks and emphases
that had long fallen into neglect, and this concern was the
Christian contribution to the social readjustment. The
most important of these tasks or emphases are those that
are to be found wherever the Church is living and vital,
namely: the sense of the social implications of Christianity
and the social responsibilities of Christians, the concern to
win non-Christians to Christ, and the realization of the
value and necessity of the Church itself both in winning
the world for him and in nurturing the life of those who
are members of the Body. These emphases, as has been
said, were not the inventions of the nineteenth century,
they were simply a return to the emphases of the Church
in the days of its first vigor. Obviously it is not possible
to do other than select representative Christians in this
attempt to meet the world's needs, and there are many in
the century who could be chosen. The four that are here
selected, however, seem well assured of their place in the
roster of Good Christian Men.

LORD SHAFTESBURY

"I was not disobedient unto the heavenly vision"

ANTHONY ASHLEY COOPER, seventh Earl of Shaftesbury, lived in what we may call modern times, and in one of the most enlightened countries in the world. Although George III was still alive when Shaftesbury was born in 1801, when he died Theodore Roosevelt was a student at Harvard. Yet the evils Shaftesbury dealt with seem as remote as the Middle Ages. He saw England and the United States change from agricultural countries to nations whose wealth lay in their manufacturing and commerce through the Industrial Revolution. The new machinery altered all the conditions under which men worked, and it brought with it hardships that make us shudder to read of them. If we hear of torture in medieval Europe, or of men being drawn and quartered in the sixteenth century we are not surprised; people did that sort of thing then. We are horrified when we hear of things quite as bad happening in the nineteenth century. This was the way Lord Shaftesbury felt, and he set out to do something about what he heard and saw.

Shaftesbury was educated at Harrow and at Christ Church, Oxford. There is no reason to suppose that he was different from any other boy or young man in his social group, except for an incident of his school days. One day he was taking a walk when he happened to pass the churchyard of Harrow parish where a poor man was being buried. The coffin slipped and fell to the ground, bursting open and exposing the miserable body. The boy asked himself, "Can this happen simply because the man was poor and without friends?" In the next fifteen minutes, he said later, he decided upon his career; and a tablet on the wall of the Old Schools at Harrow testifies to the fulfillment of his boyhood resolution:

"Near this spot Anthony Ashley Cooper, afterwards the Seventh Earl of Shaftesbury, K.G. while yet a boy in Harrow School saw with Shame and Indignation the Pauper's Funeral which helped to awaken his lifelong Devotion to the Service of the Poor and the Oppressed."

In 1826 at the age of twenty-five he entered Parliament, having obtained his seat from his grandfather, the Duke of Marlborough, who controlled numerous "pocket boroughs," for which he could send whom he would to Parliament. When the Duke of Wellington became Prime Minister, Shaftesbury was made a governor of the East India Company, the body which governed the Indian Empire. In 1834 Sir Robert Peel made him a lord of the Admiralty. Because of his family connections, as well as his personal ability and character, it may be assumed that a brilliant political future was open to him. He had decided to do something else, however. In 1828 he had served on an unimportant Parliamentary committee to inquire into the treatment of lunatics. A hundred years ago the insane and those with mental afflictions were imprisoned in cells, chained, and often lashed, and publicly exhibited to the curious, who regarded them either with amusement or with horror. Cure was completely unthought of. Lord Shaftesbury not only served on the committee, he personally visited these awful "asylums," and brought back sufficient evidence to introduce a bill amending the law. This was the first opportunity for him to fulfill his youthful vow. Before his death he had secured a complete reform of the so-called Lunacy Acts.

The next work he undertook was a reform of working conditions in mills, factories, and mines, with special interest in child workers. In some mills, in 1839, there was no age limit of employment, and the working hours were 4 A.M. to 12 P.M., a total of twenty hours. Often the children employed would not go home at all during the twenty-four hours, but lie down on the floor among the machines. These children, however, worked above ground with at least some sunlight; whereas in the coal mines boys and girls, six or even five years old, for twelve-hour periods, were harnessed like dogs to coal carriages and drew them to and fro in the damp earth. Others used to stand for the same amount of time ankle-deep in water, pumping out the mine pits. Sometimes the passages were so low that even the smallest had to spend half the working day, which for them, too, was twelve hours long, on all fours pushing the carts through the tunnels. To enumerate the industrial horrors of 1840 would read like a description of a prison of the medieval Inquisition. In 1842 Lord Shaftesbury succeeded in having a law passed forbidding the employment underground of women, and children younger than thirteen. In 1847 he put through a bill for a ten-hour day, against great opposition, even the Prime Minister refusing his support.

Another work which Shaftesbury organized and established was the "Ragged Schools." These were meant to save poor boys from a life of crime. In 1851 he told the

House of Lords that he "attributed to the miserable condition of the homes of the poor, two-thirds of the prevailing disorder." The Lodging House Act, which he sponsored, Charles Dickens, the novelist, called "the best piece of legislation that ever proceeded from the English Parliament." Dickens himself was a great worker for social reform and wrote many of his novels with that in mind. On his estate at Wimborne St. Giles, in Dorsetshire, Shaftesbury built a model village. Each cottage had all the living conveniences of the day, a quarter of an acre for a garden, and rented for only a shilling a week. Shaftesbury was also able to break up the system of virtual child slavery whereby small boys were forced by their masters to climb chimneys and sweep them from the inside. These were the "climbing boys" of which Charles Kingsley wrote in *Water Babies*. Not until 1875 did the Chimney-sweeps Bill finally end the practice, but for many years Shaftesbury as president of the Climbing Boys' Society had collected evidence of manslaughter and the actual purchase and sale of children. In 1862, in recognition of his devotion to the cause of the poor and oppressed, he was made a Knight of the Garter, the highest honor which can be awarded in the gift of the British Crown to a nobleman.

Lord Shaftesbury was a devout and earnest Christian, who was accustomed to pray before any important undertaking, and who attended church regularly. Moreover he took an interested part in organizations and movements that were inspired by the Church or by Christians. He was active in the Y.M.C.A. and in the London City Mission, and originated a movement for holding services in theatres and music halls, in an effort to remove from worship the atmosphere of formalism and mere respectability. He acted as president of the British and Foreign Bible Society for many years, and supported the missionary work of the Church.

Lord Shaftesbury had great faults. He is said to have had no tact, he was conservative and aristocratic by nature, and he was not a popular leader. Nor was he far ahead of his time; most of his achievements were cures of existing social disorders, he worked for the oppressed rather than with them. He was strongly opposed to labor unions; yet he was always regarded as their friend by the poor and the down-and-out. In 1848 the London mob was known to be plotting a serious outbreak against the government and men of wealth, and Lord Shaftesbury was asked to use his influence to prevent it. He called the City Mission to help him, and for weeks together they made every effort to still the angry passions of the crowd. When the panic was over, and things were quiet, Sir George Grey, the Home Secretary, thanked Lord Shaftesbury and the City Mission for what they had done. His relations with the poor of London and their confidence in him was revealed most interestingly on the occasion of his meeting with some notorious thieves of London, forty of them it is said. They had asked him to meet them, and he agreed. Many came with their families and friends, and he seems to have exhorted them in such a winning fashion to abandon their evil ways that the greater part agreed to do so. Lord Shaftesbury did not leave it at that, however; he had no great confidence in an emotional conversion. He immediately offered to as many as would take it, the opportunity to emigrate to Australia at his expense where life could be begun anew. Most of the professed penitents are said to have accepted.

Lord Shaftesbury's life may best be summarized by quoting from Constance Smith's essay:[1] "He awakened the paralyzed public conscience of nineteenth-century England. But he did more than this. An awakened public conscience, if it is not to spend itself in futile emotion, must find a channel of expression. Shaftesbury taught it to speak with the voice of law, and the lesson which he gave to his own generation now resounds throughout the civilized world."

DAVID LIVINGSTONE

*"Other sheep I have which are not of this fold,
them also I must bring"*

"BROUGHT by faithful hands over land and sea, here rests David Livingstone, Missionary, Traveler, Philanthropist, born Mar. 19, 1813, at Blantyre, Lanarkshire, (Scotland). Died May 4, 1873, at Chitambo's Village, Ilala (Central Africa). For thirty years his life was spent in an unwearied effort to evangelize the native races, to explore the undiscovered secrets, and abolish the desolating slave trade of Central Africa, where, with his last words, he wrote: 'All I can say in my solitude is may Heaven's rich blessing come down on every one—American, English, Turk—who will help to heal the open sore of the world.' "

Such is the inscription on the black slab in Westminster Abbey, where they buried the body of David

[1]Constance Smith, "Lord Shaftesbury," in *English Social Reformers of the Nineteenth Century.*

Livingstone among England's great. His heart was buried
by the faithful hands of his black companions under a tree
in Ilala in a gesture startling in its fitness and spontaneity,
for the explorer in him never overshadowed the missionary, and his heart was always with the black men and
women held in the double grip of savagery and the slave
trade.

The atmosphere of Livingstone's boyhood home was
that of simple faith and unrelenting toil. The words of an
old man in his native village of Blantyre were among his
earliest memories, "Now lad, make religion the everyday
business of your life, and not a thing of fits and starts." At
the age of ten he began work at the task of a cotton spin-
ner, and he soon fixed a book over his loom, so great was
his desire to educate himself. Later on he was able to go to
school, and at the University of Glasgow he began the
study of medicine. At this time he had an idea of going
to China as a missionary. He offered himself to the London Missionary Society, and the Society made it possible
for him to continue his training as a doctor. One day he
met Robert Moffat, the veteran missionary, who told him
that "in Africa on a sunny morning he might see the
smoke rising from a thousand villages where the name
of Christ had never been heard," and that a man with
health and devotion might penetrate to these as yet un-
touched regions and blaze the way for missionary work.
As a result of that conversation Livingstone was ordained
a Nonconformist minister in 1840, the year he received
his medical degree, and as both clergyman and physician
he sailed for Cape Town.

Livingstone found that few missionaries had tried to

reach the interior. Hence he set out on his voyages of exploration as part of his life as a missionary. As he saw it, white settlers whose dealings with the natives were guided by Christian principles would be the strongest agency to spread the gospel. By kindness and an obvious desire to be friendly he showed the natives that he trusted them. When they seemed hostile, he would make a point of placing himself in their power by going to sleep, or settling down to a meal as if in the midst of friends. A letter, not published until 1928, giving an old native's boyhood memories of his first meeting with Livingstone, records how many were afraid that he would bewitch them, but, said the writer, "he laughed, there was love in his eyes, he was not fierce." This impression made on a small Negro boy, and remembered through the years, he made on the natives everywhere, and those who were unfriendly were made so by his enemies among the slave traders.

In January, 1845, he married Mary Moffat, daughter of the missionary who had first drawn him to Africa. They set up a home in an interior village called Kolobeng with a tribe ruled over by one Sechele, who himself became a sincere Christian. Almost at once the Boers, the Dutch settlers in the Cape Colony who later founded the Transvaal and the Orange Free State, opposed Livingstone's attempt to open the interior; when he tried to stop the slave trade, they opposed him with violence. Once they attacked the village of Kolobeng during his absence and destroyed all his property, driving the natives away and seizing their cattle. They openly expressed their regrets at his absence, for they had meant to kill him also. The result of this hostility was to make Livingstone resolve to open up the interior at all costs and to find a means of approach other than the one through Boer country.

Lake Ngami was his first great discovery, reached after a long journey over a desert. He decided to set up a mission station on the lake, and even moved his family at great peril to their lives there, but fever forced them to return. He reached the Zambesi River, however, and established relations with Sebituane, chief of a confederacy called the Makololo, who aided him greatly in later work. He hoped to push on to the west coast where contact with British shipping would be easy, though the Portuguese controlled the ports. He sent his family to England for several years to regain their health and free him for extensive exploration. In a report to the London Missionary Society at this time he said,

"If I am spared for two years I may be permitted to establish a mission, and also to find a way to the sea on either the east or west coast—I hope in that time, too, to solve some interesting problems in relation to the slave trade, my full conviction being that this nefarious traffic will be abolished by the influence of Christian missions."

In November, 1853, he set out from Linyanti in the Makololo country with inadequate equipment and a native bodyguard, and at the end of May, 1854, after incredible hardships and dangers, reached the coast of St. Paul de Laonda, a Portuguese settlement, a distance of 1500 miles. He was ill and exhausted, and his stores and equipment all gone; but in September he started back to Linyanti, feeling that he must keep his promise to return his native carriers. The journey took nearly a year, though the tribes through whom they passed were for the most part friendly. After two months he set forth again with a larger body of carriers to find a way to the east coast by following the Zambesi, on a hint given him by Arab traders from Zanzibar. Before he had gone far, he discovered the great Falls, which he named Victoria after the queen. On his journey he had trouble with hostile chieftains, particularly where the Portuguese slave traders had aroused their ill-will. He arrived at Quilimane on the east coast in May, 1856, and sailed for England in July. He wrote in his Journal at this time: "I view the end of the geographical feat as the beginning of missionary enterprise."

At home he found himself famous. He was made a member of the Royal Geographical Society and was asked to address the British Association for the Advancement of Science. The royal family received him, and the City of London made him a freeman of the City, as did Glasgow. The Universities of Glasgow, of Oxford, and of Cambridge gave him honorary degrees, and as a result of an impressive, though by no means eloquent, speech at Cambridge, the Universities Mission to Central Africa was created. In the time which he could snatch from public gatherings he wrote *Missionary Travels and Researches in South Africa,* a book which was immediately circulated. Half of the profits from this went to finance the next journey to Africa; the rest was deposited for his family's benefit, though later lost in the failure of the bank.

He sailed again for Africa in March, 1858, this time under the government's authority as a consul for the east coast. Though the Zambesi proved impassable, finally in August, 1859, a route was found to Lake Nyassa, never before seen by white men. He pushed on to the Makololo country, only to find that all the missionaries sent out by the London Missionary Society while he was in England had succumbed to fever. The same fate was later to overtake the Universities Mission, which came in January, 1861, under the leadership of Bishop Mackenzie. A new boat was brought out from England, and together Livingstone and the bishop began explorations to find a suitable place for a station.

Relations with the Portuguese became strained, for Livingstone made no pretense of condoning the slave traffic, signs of which were everywhere—skeletons, dead bodies, and terrified inhabitants. Livingstone estimated that not more than one tenth of the slaves ever reached the coast. He soon decided that they would release any captives they encountered, and inevitably this led to fighting, though usually the native drivers fled at their approach. The Portuguese complained to the British Government that the expedition was stirring up the natives. Fever carried off the bishop in 1862, and the Universities Mission was removed to Zanzibar over Livingstone's protests. He felt that the slave trade could be destroyed only by filling the country with mission stations. The hardest blow, however, was the death of his wife in April, 1862, and again it was the African fever. To cover up his sorrow, he plunged into the work with new zeal; soon he was suddenly recalled home by the government, an action due to Portuguese pressure. He decided to sell his boat to help finance a new expedition, but not on the African coast lest it be used in the slave trade. With three white men and a few natives he sailed his boat to Bombay, 2500 miles off, and, leaving it there to await sale, he started for England where he arrived in July, 1864.

Before a meeting of the British Association he exposed the evils of the slave trade in such a telling way that British public opinion was aroused, and the Portuguese government felt it necessary to make some reply. The reply was not convincing as even Lord Palmerston, the Foreign Secretary, was forced to admit. The Royal Geographical Society offered to sponsor an expedition looking to a discovery of the source of the Nile, and the government allowed Livingstone the rank of consul in territory to the north of the Portuguese. Neither the Society nor the government was generous, each allowing him only five hundred pounds, and he had to depend on friends for the rest even with the money he realized on his boat.

In Bombay on his way back to Africa he was given a great reception and material assistance. His native companions, many of them liberated slaves, turned out a worthless lot, but he set out in spirits and reached Lake Nyassa, where he found that his name and reputation for just dealing had been used by slave traders to procure slaves. To add to his troubles the carriers of his medicine chest ran off with the contents. More than anything else this loss contributed to his illness and subsequent early death, for he made the mistake of not returning at once for new supplies. They reached Lake Tanganyika in April, 1867, where the party was forced to halt because of his weakness, and he had to accept aid from Arab slavers to be able to go on. Most of his followers deserted him at this time, and he was left with five only, entirely at the mercy of the tribes through whose country he hoped to pass.

Gangs of slaves passed daily, and he was helpless to do anything about it. Yet all the time he was making scientific observations and had no thought of returning until these were satisfactory. Hostility of native tribes added to his suffering. His Journal bears constant witness to the strain of it all:

"August 8th. I became weary with the constant strain of danger, and—as I suppose happens with soldiers on the field of battle—not courageous, but perfectly indifferent whether I was killed or not."

"September 23d. I was sorely knocked up by this march. . . . In the latter part of it, I felt as if I was dying on my feet. Almost every step was in pain. . . . All the traders (slave) were returning successful: I alone had failed and experienced worry, thwarting, baffling, when almost in sight of the end."

When he arrived at the place where his stores had been left, he found they had been sold. That was October 23, 1871. Five days later his faithful Negro, Susi, came running to him crying, "An Englishman! I see him!" It was Henry M. Stanley, who had been sent by James Gordon Bennett, owner of the *New York Herald*. Livingstone had been lost, so far as Europe and America knew, lost in Central Africa for three years. Several expeditions had set out to find him, and this one was partly an advertising venture, but it came at the crucial time. A remarkable friendship sprang up between Livingstone and Stanley, and spurred Stanley later to complete the work of Livingstone in opening to civilization the Congo and Uganda country. Together they explored the northern end of Lake Tanganyika, and Stanley tried to persuade Livingstone to leave with him. The veteran refused, saying that he must have six months more at least to mark off accurately the watershed of the Nile and the Congo. Five months later Stanley's reinforcements came, under the command of an educated native, Jacob Wainwright.

When the expedition started home, Livingstone was a dying man. His faithful followers made a hammock and carried him, and the last entry in his Journal, "Knocked up quite," bears the date April 27. A week later they halted at Chitambo's Village, Ilala, and Livingstone was found dead on the morning of May 4, as well as the natives could fix the date, kneeling by the bedside with his head in his hands. The black men embalmed the body and started with it to the coast, first burying the heart at the foot of a tree. They met an expedition coming in to find him in October, 1873, and it was the natives who insisted that the body should be taken to England. In April, 1874, the public funeral took place in Westminster Abbey, with Jacob Wainwright as one of the pallbearers. He with two others, Susi and Chuma, had been brought to England to tell the story of Livingstone's last days and also of their own five months' march with his body.

Livingstone travelled probably 20,000 miles in Africa in his thirty years there, through trackless jungle often and in the face of great hardships. A companion on one of his journeys, Sir John Kirk, wrote, "He never thinks of getting back. All he cares for is accomplishing his object at any risk whatever. His absolute lack of any sense of fear amounts almost to a weakness. He would go into the most perilous positions without a tremor or touch of hesitation." He was a man of action with one consuming passion, and not always gentle about getting his way. With those who wronged the natives he was stern and uncompromising, but with the natives themselves he was kindness and understanding itself. His ambition was to leave in Africa a trail of Christian civilization which should transform the Dark Continent, and he would have laid great emphasis on the word Christian.

The simplicity and sincerity of his religious life are exemplified in a passage from his Journal, written in the face of danger: "Felt much turmoil of spirit in view of having all my plans for the welfare of this great region and teeming population knocked on the head by savages tomorrow. But I read that Jesus came and said 'All power is given unto me in heaven and in earth. Go ye therefore, and teach all nations . . . and lo, I am with you always, even unto the end of the world.' It is the word of a gentleman of the most sacred and strictest honor, and there's an end on't. . . . I feel quite calm now."

JOHN HENRY NEWMAN

"Grafted into the Body of Christ's Church"

OXFORD has sometimes been called the "home of lost causes"; it might better be recognized as the home of nearly every revival of religion in England since the University came into being. John Wycliffe was an Oxford Fellow, as was John Wesley. Sir Thomas More and John Colet were among the so-called Oxford Reformers of the early sixteenth century. In the nineteenth century a new movement, centering around the Fellows of Oriel College, Oxford, was to restore to the Church of England, and to English Christianity in general, the sense of its corporate nature and its divine commission. The best known member of this group of Oriel Fellows, and the spiritual genius of the movement, was John Henry Newman.

Newman was born February 21, 1801, the son of an English banker; his family would have been called well-to-do middle class. His mother was descended from Huguenot refugees who had come to England when the Edict of Nantes was revoked by the French Government in 1685, and the French Calvinists became the objects of persecution. The "conversion" which Newman experienced at the age of fifteen, under the influence of the Evangelicals, those followers of John Wesley who remained in the Church of England, was not considered abnormal or unduly emotional. As a boy he discovered that God speaks to the individual soul, and this discovery was in no sense forgotten when Newman came to emphasize another side of the Christian life and experience.

Newman showed great talent from his earliest years. He mastered the violin while very young, and his "fiddle," as he called it, remained one of the refuges of his spirit. He read constantly, his favorite authors being Cicero in Latin and Sir Walter Scott in English. Scott's love for the Church and the days of the Middle Ages had a real influence on Newman. As a boy Newman was shy, serious, and brilliant, and these qualities marked him throughout his life. When he was sixteen, he entered Trinity College, Oxford, and immediately won a high place in the estimate of his tutors and fellow-undergraduates. He was elected to a Fellowship in Oriel College in 1822. Newman afterwards described this distinction, which was one of the most sought after prizes in the University, as the turning point of his life; the day of its announcement to him "of all days the most memorable."

In 1825, three years after his election to the Fellowship, he was ordained a priest in the English Church, and in 1828 he became vicar of St. Mary's, the University Church in Oxford. Almost at once the religious life of the undergraduates reflected the spiritual power of the new vicar. Communions increased, and the Sunday evening sermon became a never to be forgotten experience. Students of English literature call Newman's sermons masterpieces of composition, but they were something more when he preached them. The charm of his personality and his deep religious fervor permanently influenced every phase of University life. Matthew Arnold, who appreciated the power of Newman at this time, wrote of him: "Who could resist the charm of that spiritual apparition, gliding in the dim afternoon light of St. Mary's, rising in the pulpit, and then, in the most entrancing of voices, breaking the silence with words and thoughts which were a religious music—subtle, sweet and mournful?"[1] Perhaps that is the quality that the familiar painting of Newman by George Richmond has caught. One of his companions of these days, James Anthony Froude, said of his sermons years later, "Newman, taking some scripture character for a text, spoke to us about ourselves, our temptations, our experiences. . . . He seemed to be addressing the most secret consciousness of each of us—as the eyes of a good

[1]Quoted in J. Lewis May, *Cardinal Newman*, p. 7.

portrait appear to look at every person in the room."[2]

In 1832 Newman went to the Mediterranean with another Fellow of Oriel; the first leisure he had had for years, he used it to consider from a point of vantage the political and religious situation in England. He was frankly disquieted by what he knew of Church and State at home. He wrote some poetry on this voyage, little of which is remembered except the poem that has become one of the most popular hymns in the language, "Lead, Kindly Light." Written one evening as night fell on the sea, the poem expressed all Newman's uncertainty about things as they were, but at the same time his faith in God's power to lead him to some solution. In this temper of mind he returned to England, and there he found the stage set for great happenings.

Newman always gave as the date of the birth of the Oxford Movement, July 14, 1833, the day on which the famous "Assize Sermon" was preached before the Judges of the Court of Assizes by John Keble, another Fellow of Oriel. The sermon was later published under the title, *National Apostasy*. Keble was the author of a collection of religious verse, *The Christian Year*, which has furnished "Sun of My Soul," "New Every Morning Is the Love," and numerous well-known hymns. He was alarmed at this time over the proposed suppression by Parliament of ten Irish bishoprics. Fairly clearly there was no need for these bishops of the Church of England in Ireland since most Irishmen were Roman Catholics. The justice of the action was not questioned by Keble, the motives and

[2]Quoted in the introduction to the sermon of Newman's "The Invisible World," in *Selected English Sermons*, edited by Herbert Hensley Henson, p. 250.

the method were. There was an air of distinct hostility toward the Church in the legislation, and the further assumption that the Church was a mere adjunct to the State with no right to set its own house in order. Keble wanted to assert the independence of the Church in ecclesiastical and spiritual matters, an independence that had not been asserted for a century or more; and the Fellows of Oriel for the most part rallied to his support, not least among them Newman.

Moreover, the movement became at once a protest against the spiritual deadness of the Church and a search for the cause of that deadness. This was the concern that had occupied Newman's mind in the Mediterranean. The people of England had been stirred to new spiritual life by the Wesleyan revival of the century before, but the clergy and bishops had hardly been touched. In the main they had opposed Wesley and there was little spiritual life among them. Pluralism, *i.e.*, the clergy holding more than one office or position, and perhaps doing the work through an underpaid curate, was all too prevalent. Bishops habitually gave the best places at their disposal to members of their own families; an archbishop at the beginning of the century was said to have bestowed sixteen positions on seven of his relatives. This lack of concern for the real work of the Church was reflected in the life of Church members generally. On Easter Day, 1800, there were but six people present at the Communion in St. Paul's Cathedral in London. Although in parishes where the Evangelicals were strong there was a vigorous life of prayer and communions, the whole trend in religion, as in philosophy and economics, was individualistic. This emphasis moved such men as Shaftesbury and William Wilberforce to mighty social reforms; but the Church had ceased to offer any spiritual leadership to the nation, and men had ceased to find in the Church any spiritual power.

The Oxford Movement leaders were not alone in despairing for the future of the Church. Thomas Arnold, headmaster of Rugby and father of Matthew Arnold, and himself a Fellow of Oriel, though not a supporter of Keble and Newman, wrote at this time, "the Church as it now stands no power can save." His remedy was a loose federation of the religious bodies of England with no binding tie save the immediate danger of disintegration. Newman and Keble considered the spiritual apathy to be the direct result of the individualistic emphasis; they sought to reawaken the Church to a consciousness of a long neglected clause in her creeds, the common creeds of Christendom, "I believe in the Holy Catholic Church." They would place the stress on the Church as the "Household of Faith" and the "Body of Christ," as over against the Evangelical emphasis on personal religion. Yet they did not mean to belittle the personal side of religion, they simply felt the impossibility of any such religion except against the background of the Church and the Sacraments as the means by which individuals were cultivated.

The public announcement of the Oxford Movement came in the issuance of a series of *Tracts for the Times*, short pamphlets at first, in which the chief emphasis was on the Church and the Sacraments, and their place in the Christian life. Newman was the guiding spirit in this venture, and he wrote the first Tract as he was destined to write the last, the famous *Tract 90*. At the same time he was uniting his intellectual gifts with his evangelical fervor in his utterances from the pulpit of St. Mary's. The writers were soon joined by a learned scholar and clergyman, Edward Bouverie Pusey, who took over the supervision of the Tracts and himself wrote the later ones in more scholarly tone. Doctor Pusey was careful to point out that he was teaching no new doctrines, but simply those which the Church in England had all but forgotten. He said he learned what he taught about the sacrament "from my mother's explanation of the Catechism."

The writers of the Tracts immediately found themselves unpopular. Pusey was forbidden to preach in Oxford for two years though he was a Canon of the Cathedral and a Professor in the University. In the mind of ordinary men, often encouraged by the authorities, the "Puseyites," as they were dubbed, were leading the Church of England straight into the arms of Rome. Newman contended that the Church of England was the middle way, the *Via media*, between Protestant individualism on one hand and Roman authoritarianism on the other; and he held this to be the true catholic and primitive position. The Church of England held to what was valuable in both, and hence was best able to lead the nation into a spiritual rebirth. He was caught between the fires of opposition from both sides. The issue was brought to a head by the publication of Newman's *Tract 90* in 1841. In it he tried to interpret the Thirty-Nine Articles, which had been bound with the Prayer Book since the days of Queen Elizabeth, and which every priest of the Church swore to uphold. The Articles were statements of the faith and principles of the English Reformation, and many considered that they were therefore Protestant pronouncements and entirely at variance with Catholic doctrine and practice. Newman maintained that they were anti-Roman, aimed at the accretions to the ancient and primitive faith that had been abolished at the Reformation, but they were in no way anti-Catholic. Some who read the history of the English Reformation differently thought him guilty of intellectual dishonesty; one leading churchman said, "I should be sorry to trust the author of that Tract with my purse." Newman resigned his Fellowship and, in 1843, his pulpit at St. Mary's, and retired to a country parish outside Oxford, Littlemore, to think things over. He remarked to Pusey that they had trusted the bishops and "they have given way under us." After a period of uncertainty and when several of his friends had led the way, he entered the Roman Catholic Church in 1845.

Unfortunately for England generally Newman was allowed to go into semi-retirement. He was regarded with mistrust, perhaps because he had been too prominent and able, and the enterprises with which he was entrusted in the Roman Church met with a large measure of indifference and failure. His last sermon as an Anglican had been a heartfelt lament that the Church of his upbringing could not make use of him and others like him. The Church of his adoption was not able, seemingly, to do so either to the full scope of his powers. He was ordained to the priesthood of the Roman Church in 1847, and the next year introduced the Oratory of St. Philip Neri to England, himself becoming a member of that community. He was asked to undertake the founding of a Roman Catholic University in Dublin, but he found little interest in it even among Church authorities in Ireland; he leaned on other bishops and found them no stronger supports. One of his best-known works, *The Idea of a University*, he wrote for this venture, however, and the definition of a gentleman as one who "never inflicts pain" came from these lectures.

The book on which Newman's fame hangs secure is his autobiography, *Apologia pro Vita Sua*, written in 1864. It was the last thing Newman wanted to write, but Charles Kingsley, the novelist and social reformer, and also a country clergyman, renewed in print the suggestion, it might better be called an insinuation, that Newman had no personal regard for truthfulness. The *Apologia* was the answer, and in it Newman was completely vindicated. The work has become a classic in the language, unsurpassed in style by any work of the century. In 1879, after more than thirty years in the Roman Church, Pope Leo XIII made Newman a cardinal in recognition of his gifts and devotion, and his old Oxford College, Trinity, made him an Honorary Fellow and invited him back to the Common Room after so many years' enforced absence. Two other works appeared at this time from his pen, *Essay on the Development of Christian Doctrine*, and the *Grammar of Assent*. Newman died in 1883, a genius in the art of language, a seeker and a lover of truth, a saint and a gentleman.

The Oxford Movement did not collapse by any means when Newman left the Church of England. The power of his spiritual life and the idea of the *Via media* became its permanent possessions. Moreover neither Keble nor Pusey felt any need for such a step as Newman took, and they gradually won wide acceptance for the views he had shared with them. Sometimes their work is called the Catholic Revival because their great aim was to revive the sense of the Catholic, or Universal Church, which today Protestants also are coming to value more and more. Sometimes the Oxford leaders were called Sacramentalists because they strove with success to restore a love and use of the sacraments, especially the Holy Communion. What was true of communicants at St. Paul's Cathedral at the beginning of the century was not true at the end, nor even in the middle. Often the Movement was called Ritualistic or "High Church," because their secondary aim was to restore the churches and the services to something of their ancient grandeur, not merely as pleasing to æsthetic tastes, however, but as expressions of the truths they believed. No less than the Wesleys, the Oxford leaders wrote hymns, notably Frederick W. Faber, who himself became a Roman Catholic; they also translated or adapted old Latin and Greek hymns. These hymns have become the possessions of the whole Church. For the first time since the Reformation, communities of monks and nuns took their place in the Church of England and in the Episcopal Church in the United States. Finally the Church went to work in slum parishes in the cities of England, primarily to revitalize religion and the spiritual life, and then, as a result, to effect social reforms. The work of Newman and the Oxford Movement has been summed up by saying that the Church of England began again to produce saints. One could indeed call a notable roll of men and women in country parishes, in slums and depressed areas, in schools and convents, and in the mission field, whose spiritual lives were revitalized and whose consciences were challenged by Newman's devotion to the Church and the high moral demands of his Oxford sermons.

JANE ADDAMS

"The Kingdom of Heaven is in your midst"

"I SAW FOR THE FIRST TIME the over-crowded quarters of a great city at night. A small party of tourists were taken to the East End to witness the Saturday night sale of decayed vegetables and fruit, which . . . were disposed of at auction as late as possible on Saturday night. On Mile End Road . . . we saw two huge masses of ill-clad people clamoring around two hucksters' carts. They were bidding their farthings and ha'pennies for a vegetable held up by the auctioneer, which he at last scornfully flung . . . to the successful bidder. . . . He and his fellows were types of the 'submerged tenth.' . . . They were huddled into ill-fitting, cast-off clothing, the ragged finery which one sees only in East London. Their pale faces were dominated by that most unlovely of human expressions, the cunning and shrewdness of the bargain hunter who starves if he cannot have a successful trade, and yet the final impression was not of ragged, tawdry clothing nor of pinched or sallow faces, but of myriads of hands, empty, pathetic, nerveless and work-worn, showing white in the uncertain light of the street, and clutching forward for food which was already unfit to eat. . . . For the following weeks I went about London almost furtively, afraid to look down narrow streets and alleys lest they disclose again this hideous human need and suffering."[1]

[1] *Twenty Years at Hull House*, p. 66.

This is Jane Addams' own account of how she came to devote her life as she did to the service of humanity. As with Lord Shaftesbury the social evils of the nineteenth century burned themselves on her conscience; but it was a vision of men's needs in the places where they lived that came to her, rather than in the conditions under which they worked. She was not neglectful of the need for reform in labor conditions, as we shall see, but the city slums presented the primary problem. Her vision and the example she followed came to her in London, but she transferred them both to her own country with notable success. She opened a new field of work in America, and trained or inspired most of those who, following her, entered that field; and her name has become a perpetual challenge to all those who give themselves to the service of their fellowmen.

Jane Addams was born in Cedarville, Illinois, in 1860. Her mother died when Jane was still an infant, and her childhood centered in her Quaker father, gifted with two Quaker traits—personal integrity and a profound respect for the opinions of others. Once he told his daughter, in answer to a knotty question she put to him, "not to pretend to understand what one did not understand, and to be honest with oneself inside, whatever happened." He had been in the Illinois legislature with Abraham Lincoln, and a close friendship between the two men had resulted. The tragedy of the President's death and of the era in American history that followed the Civil War deeply affected Miss Addams' early years. She considered her hero worship for Lincoln one of the dominant influences of her life.

At the age of seventeen she entered Rockford Seminary which became in 1881, the year after her graduation, Rockford College. In 1882 she received her degree, one of the first to be awarded by the new college. In her autobiography, *Twenty Years at Hull House,* published in 1910, she tells how at college she began to read the Greek New Testament with the Greek teacher for an hour every Sunday, gaining thereby an insight into the Gospels and a love for them. In this small Midwestern college at the end of the nineteenth century there was much interest in foreign missions, and Miss Addams was often urged to consider becoming a missionary. She did not feel she could do this, but before the end of her course she had decided to study medicine and "live with the poor." With this aim she entered the Woman's Medical College in Philadelphia. A spinal curvature which had troubled her since childhood grew more serious at this time, however, and she was forced to give up her studies. For six months she was "literally bound to a bed."

When Miss Addams was able to move around again, she was advised to go to Europe for travel and relaxation. She arrived in London in the midst of the excitement caused by a series of articles which appeared in the *Pall Mall Gazette* in 1883, with the title "The Bitter Cry of Outcast London." She paid the visit, recorded above, at this time and felt afresh that she must use her learning in the service of needy men and women. Supposedly studying art in London she wrote that she became particularly interested in the drawings of the sixteenth century German, Albrecht Dürer, but

"in the most unorthodox manner, merely as human docu-

ments. I was chiefly appealed to by his unwillingness to
lend himself to a smooth and cultivated view of life, by
his determination to record its frustrations and even the
hideous forms which darken the day for our human imagination. . . . I believe that his canvasses . . . were sur-
charged with pity for the downtrodden."[2]

In 1888, while again in Europe, Miss Addams dis-
closed to her friend and companion, Miss Ellen Gates
Starr, a scheme that "had become convincing and tangible"
and by which they could apply their college training to
human need. They had both come into contact with Toyn-
bee Hall, the first "settlement house" in London founded
by the Reverend Samuel Barnett in connection with his
slum parish in the notorious Whitechapel district. Miss
Addams spent five months in the house to learn something
of the methods of work as well as to absorb some of the
spirit of the enterprise. The next year she and Miss Starr
began to search for a suitable house in Chicago in which
to start a similar work. After long weeks they found a
once large country mansion now completely surrounded
by crowded city streets and a large foreign population.
The house, which they called Hull House from the name
of the builder and original owner, on the corner of Halstead and Polk Streets, was then flanked on one side by a
saloon and on the other by an undertaking establishment.
The two women went to live there with the stated purpose "to provide a center for the higher civic life, to insure
and maintain educational and philanthropic enterprises,
and to investigate and improve the conditions in the industrial district of Chicago." That was September, 1889.

[2]*Twenty Years at Hull House*, p. 75.

Miss Addams stayed there for forty years, until Hull House had become one of the best-known institutions of its kind not only in this country but in the world.

The life and work at Hull House have been marked by variety and adaptability. Miss Addams often pointed out how the population around Polk and Halstead Streets changed from year to year; the Jewish young people wanted debates and literary pursuits, after them came Greeks who were interested in athletics, and Mexicans who chiefly wanted music classes. Hull House tried to meet each demand as it came. The first surveys of women and children in industry, of industrial diseases, and of such similar problems were made either wholly or in part by members of Hull House. Chapter headings in *Twenty Years at Hull House* also reveal that the occupants were not entirely concerned with the kind of social work that may be called ambulance service, patching up the wrecks left by modern industry and city life: "Pioneer Labor Legislation in Illinois," "Immigrants and Their Children," "Socialized Education," "Problems of Poverty." The first head of the Children's Bureau of the Department of Labor of the United States, Miss Julia C. Lathrop, and her successor, Miss Grace Abbott, were both residents of Hull House at one time.

During the War of 1914–1918 Miss Addams was an outspoken pacifist who believed that war was not the way to settle disputes between nations; yet she would not allow the House to be used for meetings that might seem unpatriotic. In an interview given shortly before her death, she said:

"Not everybody knows it, but Hull House residents

were far from being unanimously pacifist. . . . In fact, most of the residents were for the war. So were the trustees. At one meeting even, one of our heaviest subscribers announced that he would never again give a cent to Hull House as long as I was connected with it because of my views on peace. Of course I offered my resignation. But Charles L. Hutchinson said: 'Hull House has received a great deal of money on account of Miss Addams, and we have taken it. If she loses some money for us, we will just take that, too.' So nothing more was said of my resignation."[3]

After the war she threw herself into every cause that seemed to insure against another war, and in 1931 she was awarded the Nobel Prize for her work in the promotion of international peace.

At the age of twenty-five Miss Addams had joined the Presbyterian Church in Cedarville. She gave expression to her deep religious faith when she described that event later:

"While I was not conscious of any emotional conversion, I took upon myself the outward expression of the religious life with all humility and sincerity. . . . I had been brought up to the conclusion that 'sincerely to give up one's conceit or hope of being good in one's own right is the only door to the Universe's deeper reaches.' . . . I was conscious of no change from my childhood's acceptance of the teachings of the gospels, but at this moment something persuasive within me made me long for an outward symbol of fellowship. . . . There was also growing within me an almost passionate devotion to the ideals of democracy, and where in all history had these ideals been so thrillingly expressed as when the faith of the fisherman and the slave had been boldly opposed to the accepted

[3]Devere Allen, *Adventurous Americans*, p. 147.

moral belief that the well-being of a privileged few might justly be built upon the ignorance and sacrifice of the many?"[4]

The same faith was expressed when, in 1892, she read a paper before a conference of social workers in which she gave the driving force behind the founding of Hull House:

"First, the desire to interpret democracy in social terms; secondly, the impulse beating at the very source of our lives, urging us to aid in the race progress; and, thirdly, the Christian movement toward humanitarianism. . . . The impulse to share the lives of the poor, the desire to make social progress, irrespective of propaganda, express the spirit of Christ, is as old as Christianity itself. . . . The spectacle of the Christians loving all men was the most astounding Rome had ever seen. . . . It was a new treasure which the early Christians added to the sum of all treasures, a joy hitherto unknown in the world, the joy of finding the Christ which lieth in each man, but which no man can unfold save in fellowship."[5]

[4]*Twenty Years at Hull House*, pp. 78–79.
[5]*Ibid.*, pp. 122–23, 125.

Chapter 16

"THY KINGDOM COME"

"What the soul is in the body, this the Christians are in the world. . . . Christians hold the world together."

"What shall I say more?" The writer of the Epistle to the Hebrews in the New Testament asked that question honestly and not merely for effect. There was so much more to say, "Time would fail me." He had only begun to tell of the good men and true of the nation of Israel, and there were more, many more. So it is with Good Christian Men. There are more, many more. Some have lived in the past, and their deeds and heroism must go unrecorded here, must go unrecorded perhaps in any earthly register. Others are alive today, and that fact is missed by many people. The Church seems a thing of the past, its life and vitality nearly spent. Perhaps men live too close to it. They should see it at work in the difficult places. Perhaps they are waiting for a blare of trumpets and propaganda, and its best work is done away from the glare of too great publicity. As always in its history, however, the Church's vitality is best measured by the lives of the men and women who make up its membership. A brief mention of some of those will reveal how great a spirit and effectiveness there is in the Christian Church today.

Sir Wilfred Grenfell had before him as a young man the choice between the career of a successful British physician, or the life of the Labrador doctor among the fishermen of that bleak coast. He chose the latter with what results the world knows, or may read in his books, *Labrador Days*, *A Labrador Doctor*, and others. In his own words, "There never was any question as to the real object of the Mission to Deep Sea Fishermen. The words 'Heal the sick' carved in large letters adorned the starboard bow. 'Preach the Word' was on the port, and around the brass rim of the wheel ran the legend 'Jesus said, Follow me and I will make you fishers of men.'"

Today, or until recently, Toyohiko Kagawa, a "modern St. Francis" as he has been called, lives and works in the worst slum of the city of Kobe in Japan. He was born in a well-to-do family but was disinherited when at an early age he became a Christian. He chose his slum in Kobe, "where sixteen thousand people were living in eleven city blocks, as many as nine sleep in a room six feet square," because it was social reform that he wanted to effect in the name of Christ. He has become the foremost Christian of the Orient in the estimation of many, and even by the government of Japan he has again and again been recognized as an expert on social questions.

In French equatorial Africa, in the Cameroons, there has lived since 1913, with slight interruptions, a man who is among the greatest scholars of his day, Doctor Albert Schweitzer. He holds a doctor's degree in theology, philosophy, music, and medicine. When he was less than forty he had published his epoch-making book on the study of the Gospels, *In Quest of the Historical Jesus*. He had also written one of the best biographies of the musician and composer, Johann Sebastian Bach, and was to help produce the definitive edition of Bach's organ works. In 1905 by chance he saw a magazine that asked for medical aid in the Congo, and he felt it was directed to him. "I gave up my position of professor in the University of Strassburg, my literary work, and my organ playing in order to go as a doctor to equatorial Africa. Why? . . . The parable of Dives and Lazarus (Luke 16:19–31) seemed to me to have been spoken directly to us. Out there in the colonies sits wretched Lazarus, the colored folk, who suffers illness and pain just as much as we do, nay, much more, and has absolutely no means of fighting them."

The life of Charles Henry Brent, first American Bishop of the Episcopal Church in the Philippine Islands was one full of adventure and of solid achievement. Later he was made Bishop of Western New York, but his life was never limited by geography. General Pershing, whom Bishop Brent confirmed when the general was stationed in the Philippines, appointed him Chaplain General of the American Army in France during the War of 1917–1918. His great work, however, which brought him into contact with Christians everywhere, was in connection with the movement for Church reunion. He persuaded his own Church to speak and act toward that goal, and his endeavors were brought to a climax when he presided over the Conference on Faith and Order in 1927, at Lausanne in Switzerland, to which nearly every Church in Christendom sent delegates, and which did much to prepare the way for more conferences and further approaches to reunion. Bishop Brent was, with all this, a man of prayer, as his printed books of prayers show; he understood St. Benedict's words, *Orare est laborare.*

Ten years ago there died in New York a Negro named J. E. K. Aggrey, a native of the Gold Coast, educated in America, who had been a missionary to his own people and an educator in Negro schools in America. In India a member of the aristocratic Sikh religion, Sundar Singh by name, was converted to Christ in the face of family opposition, donned the saffron robe of a Sadhu (Holy man) and in the manner of St. Francis preached Christ up and down the land until he disappeared in Tibet, whence he had gone on the same mission. The first native diocesan bishop in India, Bishop Azariah, carries to the outcastes of India a Christian gospel of self-esteem, and continues to win many of them for Christ. Stories of such individuals might be told indefinitely. There is a long train of them today as well as yesterday.

Another index of the life that is in the Church is to be seen in the gatherings of Christians from all the Churches and from all over the world which have been held in the last few years. Lausanne, 1927, was mentioned in connection with the work of Bishop Brent. In 1925 a Conference on Christian Life and Work was held in Stockholm to consider the responsibility of Christians in social matters. At Stockholm and at Lausanne committees were set up that should continue the work of the Conferences, and as a result two larger Conferences were held on the same general subjects in 1937, one at Oxford and the other at Edinburgh. In 1938 the World Missionary Conference met at Madras in India. The significance of this gathering lies largely in the representatives of the young native churches

of the Orient who were present. Such a conference reveals
the life in those Churches as nothing else could and the
hope for the world there is in them. Lastly in 1939, as
Europe and the world were on the brink of another war,
representatives of the Christian youth of the world came
together in Amsterdam, fifteen hundred strong. Their
watchword was *Christus Victor,* "Christ is triumphant,"
and their closing words express the only hope for mankind, "The nations and peoples of the world are drifting
apart; the Churches are coming together."

The Report of the delegates to the Madras Conference sounded the proper note on which to end what has
been said in this book. "In broken and imperfect fashion,
the Church is even now fulfilling its calling to be within
itself a foretaste of the redeemed family of God which
He has purposed humanity to be." And again, "By faith,
but in deep assurance, we declare that this body which
God has fashioned through Christ cannot be destroyed."
This is what St. Augustine was saying in the *De Civitate
Dei,* this is the faith of Christians in every hour of crisis
for the Church. Doctor H. P. Van Dusen, in his book *For
the Healing of the Nations,* a survey of Christian work in
the Far East and an estimate of the Madras gathering,
has words that ought to be quoted here:

"In the second century of our era, an unknown Christian wrote a letter to his friend Diognetes in which oc-
curred this remarkable statement, 'Christians hold the
world together.' As imagination recalls the world of the
second century, we recognize that that was no report of
fact. Rather it was a prophecy of faith. . . . However, in
the centuries following when Græco-Roman civilization

crumbled and the Dark Ages engulfed all that mankind had created of art, learning and culture, the only institution with sufficient inherent vitality, cohesion and resolution to survive universal disintegration was the Christian Church. . . . It may be that when the judgment of history looks back upon these troubled times which are our fate, it will declare as its most important verdict upon our epoch, 'Christianity held the world together.' "[1]

[1]Pp. 198–99.

BOOKS FOR REFERENCE AND FOR FURTHER READING

GENERAL

Bevan, E., *Christianity*. Harper.

Browne, A. B., *The Way and the Faith*. Macmillan.

Clarke, C. P. S., *A Short History of the Christian Church*. Longmans.

Dawson, C., *Medieval Religion*. Sheed and Ward.

Dawson, C., *The Making of Europe*. Sheed and Ward.

Deansley, Margaret, *History of the Medieval Church*. Methuen.

Jones, C. D. (Editor), *Outline of Church History: Broadcast talks by selected English scholars*. Allen and Unwin.

Laux, J. J., *Church History*. Benziger.

Martindale, C. C., *What Are Saints?* Sheed and Ward.

Moss, H. St.L. B., *The Birth of the Middle Ages*. Oxford.

Richardson, C. C., *The Church Through the Centuries*. Scribner.

Somervell, D. C., *A Short History of Our Religion*. G. Bell.

Walker, Vera, *A First Church History*. Student Christian Movement Press.

Walker, Williston, *Great Men of the Christian Church*. University of Chicago Press.

Walker, Williston, *History of the Christian Church*. Scribner.

Wand, J. W. C., *History of the Modern Church*. Methuen.

Washburn, H. B., *Men of Conviction*. Scribner.

Watt, Hugh, *Representative Churchmen of Twenty Centuries*. Doran.

CHAPTER ONE

Alington, C. A., *A New Approach to the Old Testament*. Harper.

Robinson, H. W., *The Old Testament, Its Making and Meaning.* (Chapter Five, "Prophecy and Apocalyptic.") Cokesbury.

Rowley, H. H., *Israel's Mission to the World.* Student Christian Movement Press.

CHAPTER TWO

Foakes-Jackson, F. J., *Life of St. Paul.* Richard R. Smith.

Glover, T. R., *Paul of Tarsus.* Harper.

Inge, W. R., *Outspoken Essays.* (Volume I, Essay on St. Paul.) Longmans.

Mathews, Basil, *Paul the Dauntless.* Revell.

Nock, A. D., *St. Paul.* Harper.

Scott, C. A. A., *St. Paul: the Man and the Teacher.* Macmillan.

CHAPTER THREE

Bigg, Charles, *The Church's Task in the Roman Empire.* Oxford.

Glover, T. R., *The Conflict of Religions in the Early Roman Empire.* Scribner.

Glover, T. R., *The Influence of Christ in the Ancient World.* Yale University Press.

Glover, T. R., *The World of the New Testament.* Macmillan.

Lecky, W. E. H., *History of European Morals.* D. Appleton-Century.

CHAPTER FOUR

Browne, A. B., *The Way and the Faith.* Macmillan.

Gardner-Smith, Percival, *The Church in the Roman Empire.* Macmillan.

Mackay, H. F. B., *Saints and Martyrs.* (Especially Cyprian, and Athanasius, in Chapter Five below.) Morehouse.

Mason, A. J., *Historic Martyrs of the Primitive Church.* Longmans.

Sienkiewicz, Henryk, *Quo Vadis?* Little, Brown.
Workman, H. B., *Martyrs of the Early Church.* Epworth.

CHAPTER FIVE

Jones, Rufus M., *The Church's Debt to Heretics.* Doran.
Stanley, A. P., *Lectures on the History of the Eastern Church.* Dutton.

CHAPTER SIX

Figgis, J. N., *Political Aspects of St. Augustine's City of God.* Longmans.
Harnack, Adolf von, *The Confessions of St. Augustine.* (In *Monasticism.*) Putnam.
McDougall, Eleanor, *St. Augustine.* Harper.
Montgomery, W., *St. Augustine, Aspects of His Life and Thought.* Hodder.
The Confessions. Translated by Charles Bigg. Methuen.
    Translated by E. B. Pusey. J. M. Dent.

CHAPTER SEVEN

Butler, Cuthbert, *Benedictine Monachism.* Longmans.
Cabrol, Fernand, *St. Benedict.* Burns.
The Rule of St. Benedict. Translation with Introduction by Cardinal Gasquet. Methuen.
Workman, H. B., *Evolution of the Monastic Ideal.* Epworth.

CHAPTER EIGHT

Binns, L. E., *Innocent III.* Methuen.
Dawson, C., *The Making of Europe.* Sheed and Ward.
Dudden, F. H., *Gregory the Great.* Longmans.
Macdonald, A. J. S., *Hildebrand.* Methuen.
Thorndike, Lynn, *History of Medieval Europe.* Houghton.
Walsh, J. J., *The Thirteenth, Greatest of Centuries.* Fordham University Press.

Workman, H. B., *The Church of the West in the Middle Ages.* Epworth.

CHAPTER NINE

Chesterton, G. K., *St. Francis of Assisi.* Doran.

Cuthbert, Father, *Life of St. Francis of Assisi.* Longmans.

Housman, Laurence, *Little Plays of St. Francis.* (Two Series.) Small.

Jorgensen, Johannes, *St. Francis of Assisi.* Longmans.

Little Flowers of St. Francis of Assisi. Translated by D. R. Hudleston. Benziger.

Robinson, Paschal (Editor), *Writings of St. Francis.* Dolphin Press.

Sabatier, Paul, *Life of St. Francis of Assisi.* Scribner.

CHAPTER TEN

Chesterton, G. K., *St. Thomas Aquinas.* Sheed and Ward.

Workman, H. B., *John Wycliffe.* Oxford University Press.

Workman, H. B., *The Dawn of the Reformation.* Epworth.

CHAPTER ELEVEN

Booth, E. P., *Martin Luther, Oak of Saxony.* Round Table.

Lindsay, T. M., *History of the Reformation.* Scribner.

McGiffert, A. C., *Martin Luther, the Man and His Work.* D. Appleton-Century.

CHAPTER TWELVE

Boehmer, Heinrich, *The Jesuits.* Translated by P. Z. Strodach. United Lutheran.

Sedgwick, H. D., *Ignatius Loyola.* Macmillan.

Spiritual Exercises, with Commentary and Directory. Edited and Translated by W. H. Longridge. Scott.

Van Dyke, Paul, *Ignatius Loyola.* Scribner.

Yeo, Margaret, *St. Francis Xavier,* Macmillan.

CHAPTER THIRTEEN

Muller, J. A., *Stephen Gardiner and the Tudor Reaction*. Macmillan.

Parsons, E. L., and Jones, B. H., *The American Prayer Book*. Scribner.

Patterson, M. W., *History of the Church of England*. Longmans.

Pollard, A. F., *Thomas Cranmer*. Putnam.

Proctor, F., and Frere, W. H., *History of the Book of Common Prayer*. Macmillan.

Trevelyan, G. M., *History of England*. Longmans.

Wakeman, H. O., *Introduction to the History of the Church of England*. Macmillan.

CHAPTER FOURTEEN

Eddy, Sherwood, and Page, Kirby, *Makers of Freedom*. Doran.

Herford, Brooks, *Story of Religion in England*. Unitarian S. S. Society.

Plummer, Alfred, *The Church of England in the Eighteenth Century*. Methuen.

Vulliamy, C. E., *John Wesley*. Scribner.

CHAPTER FIFTEEN

Addams, Jane, *Twenty Years at Hull House*. Macmillan.

Addams, Jane, *The Second Twenty Years at Hull House*. Macmillan.

Bready, J. W., *Lord Shaftesbury*. Allen and Unwin.

Campbell, R. J., *Livingstone*. Dodd, Mead.

Dark, Sidney, *Cardinal Manning*. Duckworth.

Jenkins, Claude, *Frederick Denison Maurice and the New Reformation*. Student Christian Movement Press.

Martin, Hugh (Editor), *Christian Social Reformers in the Nineteenth Century*. Student Christian Movement Press.

May, J. L., *Cardinal Newman*. Longmans.

CHAPTER SIXTEEN

Axling, William, *Kagawa*. Harper.

Christus Victor: Report of the World Conference of Christian Youth, 1939. Macmillan.

Grenfell, Wilfred, *A Labrador Doctor*. Houghton.

Grenfell, Wilfred, *Forty Years for Labrador*. Houghton.

Grenfell, Wilfred, *What Christ Means to Me*. Hodder.

Hunter, A. A., *Three Trumpets Sound*. Association Press.

Kagawa, Toyohiko, *Christ and Japan*. Missionary Education Movement.

Kagawa, Toyohiko, *Love the Law of Life*. Student Christian Movement Press.

Schweitzer, Albert, *More from the Primeval Forest*. Holt.

Schweitzer, Albert, *On the Edge of the Primeval Forest*. Holt.

Schweitzer, Albert, *Out of My Life and Thought*. Holt.

Tiltman, M. K., *God's Adventurers*. Harrop.

Van Dusen, H. P., *For the Healing of the Nations*. Scribner.

INDEX

Abelard, 107, 131
Acts of the Apostles, 8, 12, 14, 15, 17–18, 35, 39
Addams, Jane, **238-244**
Aggrey, J. E. K., 248
Albert the Great, 130
Alcuin, 94
Alexander II, Pope, 98
Ambrose, St., Bishop of Milan, 59, 63
Amos, 3
Anthony, St. (of the Desert), 61, 63
Antioch, 10, 11
Apologia pro Vita Sua, see Newman, John Henry
Apostles, the, 8
Aquinas, St. Thomas, **129-133**
Arius, 44–46, 49–52
Arnold, Thomas, 233
Assize Sermon, 231
Athanasius, **42-54**
Attila the Hun, 87
Augsburg, the Peace of, 157; Confession, 159, 161
Augustine, St., **55-71**, 97, 150, 189–190, 249; *Confessions of*, 55, 65, 69, 71; *De Civitate Dei*, 68–69, 97, 249
Augustine of Canterbury, 89–90, 93
Augustus, the Emperor, 22
Authorized Version, *see* Bible, Versions
Azariah, Bishop, 248

Bacon, Roger, 105, 123
Banquet of the Lady Poverty with the Brothers, 126–127
Barbarossa, Emperor, 109
Barnabas, 10, 11, 15, 39
Becket, Thomas à, 100–101, 141
Bede, The Venerable, 83, 89, 90, 94
Benedict of Nursia, St., **72-85**, 87, 248; Rule of, 76 ff.
Bernard of Clairvaux, St., 140
Bernard of Clugny, St., 140
Bible, Versions of the, Authorized, 197; Coverdale, 187; Cranmer's, 187; Douai, 175; King James, 197; Rhiems, 175; Septuagint, 23, 46;

Tyndale, 187, 197; *Vulgate*, 67, 137, 175, 187; Wycliffe, 137, 197
Boniface, St., 94, 96
Boniface VIII, 134
Book of Common Prayer, 188–192
Brent, Bishop Charles Henry, 247–248

Calvin, John, **159-164**; *Institutes* of, 160–163
Canisius, Peter, 175
Canossa, 99
Canterbury Tales, see Chaucer, Geoffrey
Canticle of the Sun, see Francis of Assisi
Carmelite Order, 166
Catholic Revival of Ignatius Loyola, 165; or Oxford Movement, 257
Charlemagne, 94, 96–97
Chaucer, Geoffrey, 141
Cistercian Order, 84
Clarendon, Constitutions of, 101
Claver, St. Peter, 177
Clugny, Abbot of, 84; Abbey of, 98
Coke, Thomas, 209
Colet, John, 144, 228
Colloquies, Marburg, 155
Columba, St., 93
Columbanus, 93
Communion, Holy, 40, 132, 191, 237
Conference, Amsterdam, 249; Edinburgh, 248; on Faith and Order, Lausanne, 247–248; First Methodist, 207; Hampton Court, 197; Life and Work, Stockholm, 248; Madras, World Missionary, 248–249; Oxford, 248
Constance, Council of, 135, 138, 157
Constantine, 42, 44, 49
Constantinople, Patriarch of, 88, 91, 104
Cooper, Anthony Ashley, *see* Shaftesbury, Lord
Corinth, St. Paul at, 16
Corinthians, First Epistle to the, 19
Cornelius, the Centurion, 9, 24